Inside Marilyn Monroe

Inside Marilyn Monroe

A Memoir by

John Gilmore

FERINE
BOOKS

Los Angeles

Cover and Book Design by Timothy H. Kepple
Editing by Marijon Shearer
Manufactured in the United States of America
Published by Ferine Books
Los Angeles, California
Ferine Books are available to bookstores through their primary
distributor: SCB Distributors, 15608 South New Century Drive, Los
Angeles, 90248, California.
Phone 800-729-6423 FAX: 310-532-7001.
Email: scb@scbdistributors.com Website: www.scbdistributors.com

United Kingdom Distributors: Turnaround Distribution, Unit 3
Olympia Trading Estate, Coburg Road, Wood Green, London B22 6TZ
Phone: 0181 829 3000 Fax: 0181 881 5088

First Edition

Bibliographic Information for Library of Congress
Cataloging-in-Publication Data

Gilmore, John, 1935-
Inside Marilyn Monroe: A Memoir/John Gilmore – 1st ed.
1. Monroe, Marilyn, 1926-1962.
2. Motion picture actors and
actresses-United States-Biography—Memoir

ISBN 0-9788968-0-7

10 9 8 7 6 5 4 3 2 1

For my son, Carson Gilmore,
and my daughter, Ursula Maura Gilmore

Table of Contents

O, Time
Be kind.
Help this weary being
To forget what is sad to remember.
Loose my loneliness,
Ease my mind,
While you eat my flesh.

Marilyn Monroe

Author's Note

The more I knew, the deeper it went, like a wound covering itself to heal. I did try to heal—to understand. It was a dark time. Trying only pushed the loss deeper and then I found it everywhere in myself. Each event that occurred became a mirror framing her face.

A worldwide enterprise rakes profit from conspiracy theories and from manufactured exhibits of items supposedly related to Marilyn. An infestation turned epidemic. I have said, "That never belonged to Marilyn," and "That never happened to Marilyn..." So sensing now some personal need to counter the commerce of non-Marilyn endeavors called Marilyn, perhaps shedding a little realism into the jungle of fancy, I've undertaken to show this person behind the image, to make Marilyn real again if only in memory, and to share this view with others who care to gaze more deeply than passing a garish billboard.

This book then is intended to explore some personal aspects of Marilyn, gathered from my experiences of her company and from others who shared that same experience. For almost two generations I've kept notebooks, journals, scribbles on paper placemats or scraps grabbed fast so I wouldn't forget what I'd witnessed or was told. I've done this most of my life—while an actor from an early age (resigning that career following Marilyn's early death), and then long after becoming a writer.

The reconstruction of scenes, conversations and interviews contained here has been distilled from those notes, memory, reel-to-reel tapes or cassettes, the activity continuing over decades into the present. A movie set between takes proves an unlikely spot for an interview, but when an opportunity arose I seized it. I have undertaken whenever possible to document these exchanges as accurately as I could, attempting to preserve the content. Many original materials copyrighted by the author are with the John Gilmore Papers in the Special Collections Department of the UCLA Research Library.

I never envisioned writing about Marilyn, not about that personal connection to her nor about how that connection affected me as we intersected over a decade through the Hollywood and New York circuit; Marilyn wholly, hungrily drawn to art and coming to terms with her talents. I have lived my life in art, not in commerce. Nor have I expected to live as long as I have, for I hoped to seek the truth of a thing, as the poet Rainer Rilke put it, the *ding an sich*—the thing in itself. Worrying it to the nub and trying to make discoveries sometimes catapults one into harm's way.

In line with that, I'm almost apologizing for this offering on Marilyn, a gathering of fragments and scraps stretching loosely the length of her life drawn primarily from what I knew first-hand, and from piecing a patchwork picture and reconstruction through a myriad of witnesses, guesses and historical speculations from others.

It is in a vein of exploring that I've composed this memoir hoping those seeking shreds of a more human approach to the subject might find an approximation of what Marilyn was really like, and possibly gain an understanding of the reasons she did what she did, lived as she lived—as short a life as it was.

I am not presenting a concept of Marilyn's cultural significance or a detailed analysis of her movies. Nor is this a treatise on who Marilyn loved or might've loved or not loved, for in truth she was intrinsically incapable of giving or receiving love.

She was inadvertently bent toward self-denial, driven by fears so deep and troubling her life became hopelessly congested. The only escape from debilitating and often unbearable psychic and physical pain was through some form of anesthesia that numbed, though less and less did anything to alleviate the impacted core.

I have sketched her family background to track the path of how their lives affected Marilyn's. My own life is some lesser parallel to this regrettable history in its formation of an inability to love, thus the resultant play-acting through life. Marilyn's family, riddled with insanity, fostering the lack of emotional stability, bound her inwards like the limbs of a deliberately shrunken tree.

Through this inability Marilyn and I formed an unspoken link the times we crossed paths. Exploring this past to the degree I have, I recognize the axis that drove Marilyn, hounded her, and birthed an impulse to escape into herself, rather than from herself.

A more detailed account of Marilyn's career and her place in history are to be found elsewhere. I have, rather, chosen a somewhat serpentine path in exploring the emotional core that singularly propelled Marilyn through thirty-six years of life. I confess some misgiving and a sense of loss in offering this personal view some forty-five years since the last time I saw Marilyn, and consequently come belatedly out of the past with what I've carried—only now, older, understanding, I'm impelled to present this portrait of one of the most lovely yet complicated humans to have graced the planet.

My initial thanks to Ian Ayres of the French Connection Press of Paris, who set me on this course, knowing my personal links to Marilyn that I never intended for a media saturated with profit-seeking and sensation. What the media portrays is so ridiculously entrenched in caricature that any true reflection of Marilyn has been shadowed, her essence obscured. The person she was has slipped from us like sand—goodbye to that thing-in-itself. As with James Dean, I only stepped forward years after his death, urged to share "what he was really like," regardless of who it disturbed. Reluctantly, I produced a memoir on Dean's year and a half in Hollywood, as I knew him, and earlier in New York—those days on Broadway, the nights in cafeterias, afternoons in theatrical cattle calls, freezing mornings in cold water flats and then the Greenwich Village seasons that made it all worthwhile.

I have written other books since then, but Ian Ayres persuaded me to unpack my long-locked Marilyn trunk in an effort to understand something that's remained for me an outwardly silent subject since the death of someone so close to my heart and nature.

So many are gone to whom I am eternally indebted for sharing with me over almost two generations as I've sought to understand something I no longer think can be explained, only experienced, obliquely at that. I am pleased there are monuments to appreciate, more to come in decades or generations ahead, honoring the joy and pleasure of a remarkable talent. She gave much, and for Marilyn it was through the lens of a camera. By some osmosis or act of God she could enter the real world on our side of the looking glass. We are embraced with the happiness, the drama and the humor she left on this side of the mirror.

My thanks to the following (in memory and present): Richard Allan, Susan Strasberg, Rory Calhoun, Barbara Stanwyck, Mamie Van Doren, John Stix, Maureen Stapleton, Shelley Winters, Christopher Jones, Frank Cosaro, Curtis Harrington, Jerry Wald, Robert Bray, Raymond Burr, Mark Levin, Arthur Kennard, Albert Dekker, Lester Salkow, Otto Preminger, Sammy Davis, Jr., Kim Novak, Ernest Neilson, Patricia Newcomb, Tony Curtis, Sylvia Barnhart, Jack Lemmon, Richard Widmark, Eddie Bracken, Rand Brooks, Jody Lawrance, Kim Stanley, Geraldine Page, Harvey Keitel, Clint Kimbrough, Tomas Milan, Montgomery Clift, Dick Clayton, John Barrymore, Jr., Ann Bancroft, James Brown, Eileen Heckert, Kevin McCarthy, Don Murray, Walter Wood, photographer George Barris, Jean Howard, Roddy McDowell,

Sam Gilman, Bert Stern, Joanne Woodward, Diana Herbert Levitt, Kathleen Hughes, Stanley Rubin, Joshua Greene, and many others.

Special thanks to Roy Turner, archivist and genealogist, who waded with me through factual swamps; to Greg Shriener who keeps the candle burning, and to my son, Carson Gilmore, actor and writer, for his belief in his father. Also to my daughter, Ursula Maura Gilmore, and to Harrison Held, and to my friend from before the freeways, Sam Feldman.

My heartfelt thanks to Marijon Shearer, my editor and witness to my barnstorming for more than twenty-nine years; to Timothy Kepple for his hard work and unswerving dedication, and to Jill Ann Adams, a kindred spirit whose generosity, trust and assistance has made this voyage possible.

In September, 1962, Jean Cocteau wrote to Francoise Sagan, saying of Marilyn, "Elle était une âme brûlant lumineuse dans l'obscurité de nos périodes... C'est l'obscurité de ce temps qui s'est éteinte sa lumière." *She was a soul burning bright in the dark of our times... It is the darkness of that time that extinguished her light.* In 1985, Sagan said to me, "Je ne pense pas que Marilyn a jamais vu Paris. Peut-être un jour vous écrirez de Marilyn... Peut-être son esprit continuera à être lumineux." *I do not think Marilyn ever saw Paris. Perhaps someday you will write of Marilyn... Perhaps her spirit will continue to be bright."*

John Gilmore
Hollywood, California

Looking Back

The Marilyn Monroe phenomenon will never be figured out. She has been studied culturally and biographically to the most remote aspects, her image explored abstractly, psychologically, sociologically, even physiologically and philosophically, but Marilyn's essence holds in wonder, elusive as sunlight on a rolling wave. Myth, goddess, or saint—all of these, an incomparable enigma defying definition and extinction, and alive in the hearts of millions.

What remains of the real-life young woman Marilyn was stays sealed in peace from a troubled life—a continuum of misery, pain, and fear that froze into her as a small child and refused to thaw.

Left in her wake, her belongings—books, phonograph records, jewelry, coats and sweaters—have been catalogued, bartered, faked, bottled and broken apart for auctions and markets, right down to strands of yellow hair and fingernail cuttings, or the near-microscopic fragments of skin said to have been shed by Marilyn.

Not long ago, a frenzied scramble of enterprise led to a demand for the exhumation of her body—a proposal to break the seal on her crypt and examine her remains after almost half a century, tracking through her bones to discover some possible evidence to prove something went terribly wrong so long ago. Disguised beneath a crocodile concern, the core of this proposal sought to create distorted facts to fuel the fading conspiracy theories, thereby goosing book and movie sales for a handful of individuals. Fortunately for all touched by the undeniable magic of Marilyn's abilities, this last assault failed to launch past the red light imposed by the Los Angeles District Attorney and the L.A. County Coroner. So for the time being, Marilyn will continue to rest in peace.

But in the turbulence of our time, like hyenas tearing at a carcass, the opportunists hammer and gnaw at the subject, some professing to unravel the "mystery" of Marilyn's death. "Questionable," they chant, all facts having fled their grasp. The public isn't privileged to the truth, only second-hand opinions by checkbook journalists elbowing into the race, spouting theories in a kind of collective imagination or swiping

17

from one another like frantic pickpockets at a racetrack. What is finally presented is yet another weary mass of misinformation, stale as a wad of chewed gum.

The media has chased the caricature of Marilyn down the decades like pirates chasing a catboat of coveted currency. The chase hasn't been about the truth. It hasn't even been about what the truth might have been or could have been.

Biographer Donald Spoto didn't march in the same parade. An honest historian, his book, *Marilyn Monroe: The Biography*, is an objective work that in the main does not compromise to sensation. Late in the 1990s, Spoto interviewed me for his book on James Dean, *Rebel: The Life and Legend of James Dean*. His interest spurred me to write a second book on Dean, *Live Fast—Die Young: Remembering the Short Life of James Dean*, following a memoir I had written more than twenty years before.

Though his book on Marilyn had already been published, Spoto and I spoke briefly about her when she had an apartment on Doheny down the hill from Sunset Boulevard, the same building as actor John Hodiak. I told Spoto before I met Marilyn I'd only known about her from movies and magazines, but came face to face with her through Hodiak, a mentor in '53. I was caught not only by her stunning beauty but by a kind of shining directness—a simple openness. She was like a large, gorgeous child.

Looking exactly like she'd stepped out of a magazine gave me a hard time not falling for her instantly—whether I'd admit it to anyone or not. Others had the same reaction, I knew, but there I was, trying to look right into her eyes but I couldn't see her eyes worth a heck because of the big black sunglasses blocking part of her face. I'd read her eyes were blue with a cast of gray and I'd seen them shining a seductive, playful way from a hundred photographs, but that first time facing Marilyn was like seeing an angel. All she lacked was wings.

Not long before that day I'd met Marilyn, I'd talked to the amazing Tallulah Bankhead at a party. Being so young, I was usually a wallflower at such slick get-togethers though I didn't actually look that young, trying to appear debonair with a gin and tonic. Bankhead, draped on a leopard-skin upholstered sofa, waved me over, her gold bracelets jangling as she patted the cushion. Drink in hand, I joined her. We spent a half hour smoking and talking about *Lifeboat*—the picture she'd made for Alfred Hitchcock, Tallulah starring opposite John Hodiak. She said something like, "John is one of the most marvelous and essentially natural actors I've had the pleasure of working with. It was indeed a pleasure because he's real. He has the ability of socking them right where their balls should be." But, she said, "Unfortunately, John is actually too good for this goddamned town and possibly any other town that doesn't know when it's got a ring that isn't brass but gold." She blew out a stream of smoke and said, "Like an anteater, Hollywood cannot see beyond its fucking nose."

We also chatted about *Desert Fury*, starring Hodiak and introducing Wendell Corey. Liz Scott, Mary Astor and Burt Lancaster filled out the bill. I'd been on an interview at MGM and chanced into Hodiak talking on a pay phone at the end of a hall. He glanced at me, gave a few looks like I might've known what he was talking about or was making him nervous standing a few feet away and staring at him. I didn't know what

he was talking about but I waited until he hung up and then he gave a shrug, like he thought maybe I had understood what he'd been talking about, but I hadn't. He raised his eyebrows and I blurted out my admiration, saying how much I admired his work, and even mentioned the chat with Tallulah. He laughed, said she was quite a gal, and asked, "She tell you what I did to her on that rubber raft?"

Grinning, I kind of let on like maybe I knew what he was talking about and then he said, "You want to get a slice of New York cheesecake?"

At that small afternoon party at John's on Doheny, he asked if I'd ever met Marilyn Monroe. I said no, I hadn't. I'd never seen her in person. "She's down in the patio," he said and winked, leading me to the edge of his terrace. Clear air, bright sun. Not a cloud in the sky.

The blonde with the champagne glass in hand, laughing in the midst of a few other people, glanced up against the glare. Her teeth were sparkling, wet and catching the sun, and with her squinting up as she was, her hair glowed almost white like a halo around her head. Long, slim legs in the skin-tight, white

John Hodiak

toreadors made her seem taller than people thought she was, plus the red high-heels with open toes showing her nails bright with red polish. She

Jonathan Gilmore

didn't appear small down in the patio, not little like Gloria Swanson, but was standing straight with that ramrod presence like Joan Crawford, only beaming— that was plain fact. Marilyn radiated a glow or light like she had some radioactive core just beneath her skin. The scant white top didn't have any sleeves, and her arms and the tips of her shoulders and her neck were white like she hadn't been in the sun. It was as if the sun was somehow shining inside of her.

I had to squint and John called down, "Hello, gorgeous! What're you doing down there?" She raised her other hand to her forehead and said, "Hi, John! Why don't you come down for the party—" She said someone's name—saying it was their birthday—Fred or Ed or something.

"I've got my own party going," Hodiak told her. "You come up and join us. Bring your friends."

She said she was waiting for Ed or Fred, and John introduced me, saying, "This is Jonathan—an actor pal who's trying to be a movie star. Come on up and spill him your secrets."

I said hello to Marilyn. I said, "Hello—" or good to see you— something like that, and she said hello back. Simple as that. Hello— hello, then peering through those big sunglasses, she said to me, "Bring your friend John Hodiak down and both of you join us." She said her party was probably better than ours and she was having a marvelous time.

"Different," Hodiak said. "Different's the word, honey. Not marvelous."

"Oh, come on, John," Marilyn said. "They're all the same, aren't they?" She laughed and John wagged his finger at her.

"Yours are naughtier," he said.

"They are not naughtier," she replied. "They're just more fun!"

Fred or Ed or whoever he was showed up in tennis shorts and cardigan and joined the cluster around Marilyn.

I could never imagine her being alone, but over the years ahead I'd come to know she was alone far more than she'd ever wanted to be. Couldn't make that connection with someone to be with her, like it just didn't fit no matter who it was. Like a no man's land, you called across a gap but never got closer than the reach of your voice.

The trend in reporting about Marilyn has long been

to separate her into two individuals, one the movie queen with sex aplomb, and the other—more elusive, a withdrawn kid, a child unseen by the world but who troubled Marilyn, as if the kid had a stick with a prong that tortured her night and day because she could never hook up with anyone who ventured to cross over that trench.

It is said the two halves of Marilyn could never combine to form one whole being, and I have been guilty of proclaiming the same. I couldn't help being swayed by the propagandized, subliminal thrust of the media to ascribe a division in Marilyn's personality—an unauthorized overhaul of her psyche and her spirit.

The pretty child, Norma Jeane, nobody seemed to love or care about, was to sustain a gaping wound inside the glamour queen who changed her name and grew up. The name change didn't change who she was, nor did the dedicated work to create an image now recognized everywhere in the world. It was a stroke of genius within the machinery of Hollywood, that transformation from unhappy kid to movie star, the challenges so extreme the process had a tempering effect, like an endless heat testing that flexed her core to its extreme usability—and of course, salability.

Much later, Shelley Winters told me, "They took away her soul."

There's never been anyone like Marilyn. Possibly never again will someone hit the point of such perfection as she, as her image reflects from a silver-grained screen so many times larger than life.

So many components fuse to make success—the motion picture camera, lens, film, a concentration of lighting and synchronized sound plus the physical presence of Marilyn—a miraculous joining of many pieces of equipment and people in the making of a cinematic image. Finally, after editing, the images on this strip of celluloid are projected onto that big screen that bounces it back and Hollywood hits the jackpot—though Marilyn was always absent in collecting the payoffs.

Her changed name meant a lifetime ticket to the celluloid circus, though it meant that Norma Jeane Mortensen or Baker or Dougherty or whatever she'd wanted to call herself had adopted the name of Marilyn Monroe. The same as Tony Curtis changed his name from Bernard Swartz. Francis Ethel Gumm became Judy Garland, and the beautiful Hedy Lamarr's name replaced Hedwig Kiesler. Ruby Stevens changed her name to Barbara Stanwyck, and Veronica Lake's birth name was Constance Ockleman.

The difference in Marilyn's case was not the fitting of another name, but the absence of a father who disappeared when her life began, and a mostly absentee mother whose emotions leaked as little as a broken faucet. "A father and a mother are people you should be able to count on," Marilyn told New York director John Stix in a discussion on psychoanalysis. "Someone who will be there no matter what," Marilyn said. "And they're never going to go away... If that is not present in a person's life, then things can become unmanageable..." Stix said Marilyn stressed the point more than once as though offering an explanation for "Whatever possibly can go wrong in one's life."

Studio publicity stirred up a stew of sadness for Marilyn's childhood, one of foster homes and orphanages, mistreatment by strangers, a child reduced to slavery (as the studio would eventually reduce the same young woman to a slave contract). "Yet her beauty prevails," the pub-

licity department announced.

Marilyn liked the pitch. She elaborated upon it many times—embellishing misery, shoring up the happy moments, padding the abuse and the Little Orphan Annie plight. "...as a kid she didn't mind the orphanage so bad," Sammy Davis, Jr. told me years later. "She'd had other kids around her nonstop and that can be a blast. But she did say the first year she suffered nightmares practically every night and forced herself to stay awake by putting bits of gravel in her bed and lying on them...

"Do you think that's true?" Davis asked. "We were at a party with Dean Martin when she told me that. She was doing a picture with Dean and the studio was about to can her to salvage losses because she'd been in a bad way. Headwise she'd turned into a fucked-up mess—just so damned sad, and Dean adamantly notified Fox he wouldn't do the picture with-

out Marilyn. But they scrapped the movie anyway—and poor Marilyn. Her head had to roll. A few wanted to help her—very few because the rest were hacking off pounds of her like divvying up a side of beef."

Considering himself one of the chosen ones, Davis still swore, "Saving Marilyn was like trying to push straws through a brick."

She told interviewers she'd been molested as a child. She emphasized pains lingering from never-ending loneliness and a continual fear of abandonment. Trading dreams with John Stix, she said, "I am put on a tiny desert island that isn't any bigger than your kitchen. I know the tide is going to rise and the ocean will cover this little island, and I will sink..."

Ralph Roberts, one of the few who were close to Marilyn, said, "She was always tiptoeing to the edge of something and checking it to make sure it was safe to proceed. Some instinct to be afraid of what might be out there. I was her masseur and we spent many hours together. I was on a number of pictures with her and we sometimes shared ideas, like she thought we had a psychic link. But I have to admit I never truly was able to know Marilyn beyond the surface of her life, let alone try to understand what was going on inside her head..."

I never fell in love with Marilyn. I loved her as an open kind of connection of the spirit; so obvious and overwhelmingly felt at times I had to back off. Had nothing to do with physical desire or thoughts of intimacy. The essence was too close and too bound to our common family experiences—or lack of family experiences—and I have waited until I'm alone, with few relatives alive and no marriages or entanglements, to finally try to express the connection I felt with Marilyn, how it puzzled in on me, begging to be buried.

For me, vanity snatched my father from all major blocks of my existence, so distanced that he remained a speck on an otherwise empty horizon. I was six months old when my mother hit the road, her emotional emptiness and my father's narcissism breaking apart a four year on-and-off marriage. Perhaps a year of those four they were actually together (if you stacked the scattered months into one pile), no doubt wrangling half of that by a sorry clash of egos.

My mother, a bit player on the MGM lot and boozing pal of Jean Harlow, yearned to see her name in lights somewhere under Harlow's. She never surfaced from the shadows of day player and bit-filler, her claim to fame from *Flying Down to Rio* with Dolores Del Rio and Richard Arlen, and the sets collapsing under the Long Beach earthquake. What she had in common with Jean Harlow was a taste for the same booze and together they emptied bottles. She continued her glamour hunt for another two years after my birth in L.A. General Hospital's charity ward, until Harlow kicked the bucket under vague circumstances.

I'd already been almost two years with my paternal grandmother who I stayed with another nine years.

Marilyn, nine years ahead of me, also gave her first yell in General Hospital's charity ward, then managed to sprout like a weed in a bunch of impersonal terrains. The name "Mortensen" is scribbled on Marilyn's birth certificate, but who he was has never been documented with certainty and that loose end in her short life has stayed as mysterious to others as it was to Marilyn—an unending throb of uncertainty as unreachable as an impacted, undiscovered ache.

Her mother, a looker as well, hauled strings of mental unbalance from a past that never figured a fact without confusing it with fiction. The woman never wanted kids and soon as they plopped forth she found a way to unburden herself. Just like my own mother's abandonment of her offspring, shrugging the kid into another's hands, obsessed with the high life and hoping to gather whatever spilled over from Jean Harlow's limelight.

My mother ran with her infant for safety in El Monte but quickly returned the unwanted goods to my grandmother like an ill-fitting shoe that pinched too painfully. She'd come back for me later, she said, same as Marilyn's mom said and as countless mothers in pursuit of self-serving ends have said, escaping the conflicts of saddling self with baby—real needs demanding what can't be delivered. A door pounded on that can never be answered. The solution? Pawn the bundle, disposing of what doesn't fit in the fantasy life they envision.

For almost fifty years I've thought of Marilyn as a fellow artist caught as some endangered species in a world of commercial expediency. Her innate abilities guaranteed returns, regardless of her self-appraisal, for the slave masters raking in the profits.

People I knew, lives intersecting with Marilyn's, made up a circle I gravitated toward and found myself drifting in and out. Hollywood—New York—back to Hollywood. A very few chose to recognize in Marilyn the doubts she suffered or anxieties that ate at her self-esteem, plaguing her nights like a disease she couldn't shake. Poor Marilyn, indeed, said Sammy Davis, Jr. Sad how little her anguish was acknowledged as a debilitating handicap rather than a stamp of being as mentally unbalanced as her mother—and her grandmother, and her grandfather, and perhaps her father, whoever he was. Marilyn was a leper you couldn't recognize by the skin because all the disease was on the inside.

Whether any of us deserve anything in life, it was a clear cinch Marilyn never got to second base. Her game was over in the first inning. A private life that was a knot of denial and doubt, of sleeplessness or too much sleep, of too many drugs and alcohol poured to quell a longing to be wanted, admired, respected and loved. But Marilyn could neither receive nor give love. No one could help her. We were on the outside of that wall built of her illustrious success, separate from her person yet surrounding her—protecting her like a poison.

She was a beautiful girl with enormous talent who had no personal grounding. She didn't fit anywhere. The stage upon which she earned so much money for others and so little for herself had no floor beneath her feet. Marilyn was exploited by many and not one person could quench her longing for fulfillment. Then, caught in that solitary, suspended state of suffering, she died.

In death she has proven more valuable, profitable and enduring than in life. I venture that almost every person in the civilized world has been touched in some way by Marilyn Monroe. Yet she lived in an invisible capsule that allowed no one to reach her. The circumstances of her early abandonment clearly cemented the impossibility of happiness. She died alone, behind a closed door, with no hand to hold or voice to reach her.

I confess my timidity or selfishness for the half dozen or so times I was in Marilyn's company and never reached past her fame to engage our spirits, connected by our pasts and our failures for parents. I failed because I was intimidated by Marilyn's success. In retrospect, I can pinpoint those exact moments in her blue eyes with that cast of gray that seemed to ask, "Are you my friend?"

I wanted so much to be that person, caring without expectation, yet an inability to reach past my self-concerns shut me in my own cocoon. Perhaps I was conditioned by my late friend James Dean's maverick attitude that forced one to a magnet position, attracting rather than giving, surely distancing me from a more than an impersonal connection with Marilyn.

Had we made Jerry Wald's movie, *The Stripper*, as was projected, Marilyn and I might have been able to bridge some personal gap that was always so apparent and cumbersome. Now in retrospect am I swearing this devoted sense of friendship I've carried for a person forty-four years dead, but so alive in the vivid presentations she gave us. Though I wanted to believe there had to be shreds of love somewhere in there, who Marilyn was inside of herself has stayed as hidden as it was when I failed to be her friend.

Gladys Pearl Monroe

By Way of a Past

Marilyn's grandmother, Della Hogan, wasn't a particularly good-looking kid, but showed a considerable streak of ambition and a load of gumption. Born in Missouri in 1876, she was raised in a small, God-fearing, rural town. Yet Della's father, Tilford Hogan, a farmer, and her mother, Jennie, split up and divorced, choosing to live with disgrace rather than with one another. Della's growing-up years were divided time between her two parents, and though she was considered lively and loved to dance and sing, she didn't marry until she was twenty-two, and then to someone she said she barely knew and would possibly never understand.

Otis Elmer Monroe had traveled from Indiana to Missouri looking for better wages. He wound up painting houses, digging holes, patching roofs and marrying Della Hogan. He was thirty-six and a disappointment to his bride's folks. It wasn't the age difference that worried them, but the fact that they knew nothing about Monroe, his background, or his family. Even as they shouldered the shame of divorce, Della's folks had prayed for a better life for her. They asked why she had married Monroe. Della replied, "He's the one that asked me…"

According to old letters, Otis Monroe had a certain "wanderlust" charm, often speaking of steamships and exploring foreign countries. He wanted to see Hawaii and travel the Old Country. A yearning to do something important seemed to fester at the seat of his hopes. When drinking, he said people would someday look up to him. They'd remember him. He just never seemed to know what it was he would do to capture their attention.

Della wrote to a relative that her marriage to Otis was like "living with a shadow of someone" she didn't know. Hard as she tried, she was unable to understand him or figure out what he wanted. She was convinced he probably didn't know what he wanted, either.

Not long after the marriage, Otis was entertaining a job offer from the Mexican National Railway. It would mean relocating, moving far away. Della said she didn't care whether they went to Mexico or

Timbuktu, because she was eager to see something different than the small "show-me" town where she'd spent her life, and she saw no other options except to "suffocate" in Missouri.

Otis accepted the job and the couple traveled the Butterfield Trail to Eagle Pass, Texas. They crossed the Mexican border to settle into the hot, dusty town of Ciudad Porfitio Diaz.

Otis went to work for the Mexican National Railway and Della, sharing none of her dissatisfactions with him, created work for herself by helping the Indian and Mexican women who she felt lived like "dogs in a pig pen."

Gladys Pearl Monroe

She performed as midwife, delivering several babies until she became pregnant herself and then sat, fanning herself and reading American newspapers. On May 27, 1902, she gave birth to a girl she named Gladys Pearl Monroe, the future mother of Marilyn Monroe.

Time stumbled on in the Mexican town. Nights blazed into dawns, and each new day seemed to sour the commitment Otis had made to the Mexican National Railway. Soon he was talking about California. Everybody was going to California. A future, a place to raise a family, specifically Southern California's rapidly developing city of Los Angeles. The newspapers told of the city's expanding transportation system—the trams, streetcars and trains joining all points on the compass into "a network of progress."

Like many others after the turn of the century, the Monroe family packed their possessions and traveled to the land of "promise and opportunity..."

They rented a small apartment on West 37th Street in the south-central section of Los Angeles, between Western and Vermont avenues, and with good recommendations from Mexico, Otis went to work for Pacific Electric Railway.

Over the next two years the Monroes made friends, and Della, pregnant again, wrote that Otis seemed to be surrendering his notions of traveling around the world on a steamship.

The second baby was born, a boy they named Marion Otis Elmer Monroe. However, records are vague – if not totally missing — on the circumstances of Marion's birth.

A short time later Della told a cousin that Otis was suffering "periodic fits of dizziness" which at first she blamed on his drinking. But even sober, Otis often said he felt suddenly as though he might pass out. He complained of feeling stifled — burning up at times as if by some sort of fever, but refused to see a doctor. At other times he seemed to sink into depressions, saying he couldn't do more than he was doing— couldn't move ahead or make more money. His life was running on a "sour track..."

They moved several times, from one bungalow to another, from rooms to cheap apartments. Unstable, with little to call their own, Otis continued drinking and showing signs of a failing memory.

After renting a house at 2511 Folsom, in the Boyle Heights section of Los Angeles, Otis got a promotion to assistant foreman, and a raise. They were able to purchase a house around the corner, at 2440 Boulder Street.

Things improved for a while, but then something happened that Della neither understood nor could do anything about. Severe headaches plagued Otis, his moods fluctuating from senseless outbursts to morose stupors that seemed to shroud him for days.

Then came the seizures—the violent shaking of his limbs. He'd froth at the mouth. Little Gladys, now six years old, shrank in terror from the sight of her father's tremors—the stumbling, falling, the "shaking..." He'd cry out, cursing and yelling at shapes only he was seeing.

"I am afraid Otis is going crazy," Della wrote to her cousin. Afraid he could harm the children, she told Gladys to stay away from her father who was unable to control himself.

Gladys was handed over to the neighbors while Della attended to her deteriorating husband. He was showing signs of paralysis as though he had suffered a stroke. Realizing she could do nothing for him, and against his curses, she had him admitted to the County Hospital in San Bernardino.

The diagnosis came as a dreadful shock. Otis was suffering the final stages of syphilis. The disease had affected his brain. He was insane.

"He is so badly off," Della wrote, "there is nothing they can do and I am told he is going to die..."

Otis was moved to the California State Hospital for the mentally ill where he lingered for months, bedfast, restrained at times and finally slipping into a coma. He died on July 22, 1909, the cause of death cited as "general paresis"— insane or paralytic dementia, a disorder affecting the brain and central nervous system with accompanying psychotic symptoms.

Gladys Pearl Monroe

Della could only tell seven-year-old Gladys that her father had "gone mad." Marion was too young—too confused. Della was unable to speak the word "syphilis..." Gladys already believed her father had turned into a lunatic, and Della confirmed that he had indeed lost his mind. He could not "think right anymore..." she told Gladys. He had gone to God.

With resentment at being "stranded" with two children, Della was determined to keep the house. It was her only security. To pay the bills, she took in boarders and got help from churches and charities.

She was thirty-three, a widow with two children, and she began entertaining men, preferably widowers. The house had to be paid. The children had to eat. She couldn't do it all by herself. An ex-acquaintance of Otis from Pacific Electric, Lyle Arthur Graves, agreed with Della and proposed marriage.

Believing such a union could guarantee solvency, Della accepted. They were married in March of 1912 by a Los Angeles justice of the peace. Graves moved out of his rented flat on South Hill Street and into Della's bungalow.

While the two children shared a room, Della was soon unhappy with her second husband. He had lost his job and seemed reluctant to work. The marriage soured fast and Della lost the house. Leaving Graves, she moved into an apartment with the children and sued him for divorce, charging "failure to provide" and claiming she had "to live on the charity of friends" because Graves wouldn't work. He was in good health but remained unemployed, she said, further charging him with "dissipation and habitual intemperance."

Christmas was coming and Della had little money, not even enough to buy presents for the children. Graves hounded for a reconciliation. They didn't have to divorce, he said, they could save the marriage. He convinced Della to "give it another try," and they jointly rented another house near Union and Sixth Street, west of downtown.

Less than half a year and the reconciliation "flew out the window..." as Della wrote. Again she gathered the children and moved, divorcing Graves and petitioning the court to restore her name to Della M. Monroe.

Gladys was eleven, sometimes a cheerful child, yet dissatisfied with the constant moves, the lack of clothing, the paltry food she and her brother would be left to nibble while Della sought work, or new companionship—prospects for financial security in a troubling time. The applicants came and went, a few handsome men, but others were short with big stomachs, some older in sweaty hats and smelling bad. None of them hung around very long.

Della had moved from the downtown area, taking a house in Venice, a few blocks from the Santa Monica beach. Hopping from job to job along the oceanfront boardwalk, "making friends..."as Della put it, soon socializing with a widower she met in the expansive Venice Dance Hall on the pier.

Della Monroe and relative

After a brief time of chatting on the balcony that framed the dance hall, Della and Charles Grainger were talking about sharing a house as man and wife—in name only, Grainger insisted, for "appearances sake." He was reluctant to get married so soon, and Della agreed. The marriage to Graves had proved a disaster.

Gladys had become precocious, though at times seemed to withdraw, refusing to answer and saying nothing. It was as if the same moroseness of her late father haunted the young girl. Della wrote to her cousin,

John Baker and Gladys

"She does not answer and I wonder if she has trouble hearing…There isn't the money for a doctor."

Della's cousins had relocated to California, were living in San Diego, a half day's ride from Venice, and offered to assist in whatever way they could. A short time after the invitation, Della packed a valise of Marion's clothes, a pillowcase of his toys and sent him to stay with the cousins, promising a "grand time" for the summer in San Diego. Far better, she told the boy, than being cooped up with his "disagreeable" sister. Della told her relatives that the two children were difficult to take care of at "the present time," but Gladys was old enough to "do something to help her mother…"

While her mother encouraged Charles Grainger, Gladys nursed soda pop, ate noodles and cupcakes and stayed "tucked in" with the door locked.

When Della told her the plan for sharing a house with Grainger, Gladys didn't hide her displeasure over her mother's attentions to yet another man—another potential husband for Della and father for Gladys.

She demanded to know why Della couldn't stay with her, why Marion wasn't coming back and why she had to pretend she was happy when she wasn't.

Della didn't know what to do. She tried to explain why the support of a husband was necessary. Bills had to be paid or they would be thrown on the street. They had to have money in the bank. Grainger had a good job, she said. He worked for the oil company and often traveled to other countries, just as Otis had only dreamed about.

Gladys decided to do what she wanted whether her mother liked it or not. If Gladys was chasing after boys, Della wasn't sure, but when Gladys suddenly seemed enraptured, it was like an overnight change had occurred. Gladys had met a young man named John Baker, originally from Kentucky, who was working a concession on the pier. Twenty-six years old, John Baker claimed that he fell in love with Gladys the moment he saw her. Gladys told her mother, "John has money and he says he wants to marry me..." If she married him, she said, he'd make a home and they could build a life together.

Gladys thought Baker was the man of her dreams, but she was still too young to legally marry. There was a chance that she was already pregnant.

For Della, the chance to relieve herself of the burden of support was being handed over like a slice of beef. She said she was happy for Gladys, swore that her daughter was eighteen years of age and witnessed a quick marriage ceremony to John Baker on May 17, 1917. Della even brought a small bag of rice to sprinkle on the couple.

Jack Baker, Marilyn's half brother

Seven months later Gladys gave birth to a baby boy, though it seems the birth was not officially documented, even as births were being systematically recorded in Los Angeles County. Baker had read Jack London's *Call of the Wild* and named their son Jack, after London. A birth certificate for baby Jack, or for Robert, as he was also known, has never been discovered.

By now, Grainger (claiming to be Della's husband) shared with Della, Baker and Gladys the cottage on Coral Canal in the center

35

of Venice, a storybook interpretation of Venice, Italy. Floral-laden cottages lined the saltwater canals where gondolas taxied residents around the city. Della's financial woes appeared to have been relieved by her daughter's marriage. Baker owned a half interest in a general merchandise business, then opened another concession with Gladys on the Pickering Pleasure Pier.

Della was presenting herself as Mrs. Grainger (even obtaining a passport on November 20, 1920, as wife of Charles Grainger), though a record of the marriage seems to have never been documented. They lived together as husband and wife—on and off, Grainger in and out of Della's life—even buying real estate as a married couple, though Della's name changed back and forth between Grainger and Monroe.

Gladys became pregnant again and in 1919, she gave birth to a second child, a girl she christened Bernice Inez, but stated on the birth certificate she had never had other children.

What became of Jack—also known as Robert Jasper Baker? As Della had done with Marion, her daughter relieved herself of the baby by convincing neighbors that placing the child with them was "only a temporary situation..." as Gladys put it, due to the difficult time she was having.

The truth would come out some years later when Gladys made it clear that she never had "inclinations for motherhood..." A long-ago neighbor, Agnes Petersen, now an invalid in Phoenix, Arizona, says, "Gladys Baker did not accept the responsibility of taking care for a child. She didn't see herself as a mother and she didn't want children because it would cramp her style, though she had the children anyway." The children were left temporarily with a neighbor while the difficult time Gladys was having—not financial but marital—grew more serious by the day.

In June of 1921, Gladys sued for divorce. She could no longer tolerate his abuse, she said. He had called her "vile names, beaten and kicked" her on several occasions, even striking her on the face. "This treatment has caused extreme mental pain and injury," she charged. She had been "a good and loyal wife..."

Baker challenged her accusations, countering that Gladys had conducted herself "in a grossly lacking and lascivious way unfit as wife and mother." But nine months later the courts ruled that Gladys was entitled to a divorce.

By that spring the relationship between Della and Grainger had run dry and the bungalow on Coral Canal was abandoned. Della and Gladys leased another house on Rose Avenue in Venice, Della signing the lease "Della Monroe," not Della Grainger as she had signed previous documents. It appeared for the time being that Grainger was out of her life.

The four-room bungalow on Rose was a short walk to the ocean, and as she had in the past, Della rented out two bedrooms to supplement her wages as a housekeeper.

Having given up the concession on the pier, Baker had been granted weekend visits with the children. He was selling insurance and asked the company for a transfer to Kentucky. One weekend, with Jack and Bernice in his custody, Baker fled Los Angeles for his native state.

"I do not know how Gladys took the abduction," says a later associate and friend. "We spent time on the pier and she talked about hiring a detective. She borrowed money and then rode the train to I think Lexington, Kentucky. Then she went south to a small town above the Tennessee border where John Baker was living..."

Gladys agreed that Baker would take permanent custody. She would later say she made that decision because the children would enjoy a better life with their father than she could afford to give them.

Though they had split with the men in their lives, there was no harmony for Della or Gladys. They quarreled over money—

Grace McKee and Gladys

accused one another of stealing. How had the rent money disappeared? The two argued and fought, and their tenants got into the fights until all were evicted. The notice to vacate charged that Della Monroe had never even paid the first month's rent on the lease.

That was the first of a series of evictions and legal squabbles. Disagreements between Della and Gladys ended when Gladys moved to Hollywood.

Grainger came to Della's rescue. Using the name "Mrs. Grainger" once again, Della moved into an empty bungalow

Gladys Baker

she had co-purchased with Grainger in name only. It was in Hawthorne, east of Manhattan Beach and several miles south of Venice.

Meanwhile, Gladys told a Hollywood chiropractor she dated briefly that she had not been able to make "adjustments to have children" in her life. She said she felt bad that Jack and Bernice were so far away, but there was nothing she could do.

Gladys' brother, Marion Monroe, had settled in Salinas where he was working as a mechanic, married and starting a family. Gladys would never see her son, Jack, again. He would die of tuberculosis at fifteen years of age, and how Gladys felt about his passing has never been revealed. An acquaintance remembers Gladys as "always ready to have fun," but a "cold person" lacking a sense of care. "She seemed to have little patience or interest except in what she could momentarily content herself with. She would seem willful and hard, or maybe so confused and sensitive she had put up a front to keep from being affected by the rest of the world ..."

Learning film cutting and splicing at Consolidated Film Industries, Gladys' immediate supervisor was a slim, attractive young woman named Grace McKee. Consolidated printed and developed motion picture dailies for producers and directors and provided major studios with cutting rooms for editing and projection rooms for inspecting theater prints. Gladys soon became Grace McKee's most diligent worker. Grace was intrigued by the aloofness Gladys often displayed, which others mistook for a superior attitude.

Grace would later say, "I didn't have many close friends. I was getting a divorce and Gladys Baker had been divorced. She didn't have close friends, either, and most people were looking at their own problems or chasing after the almighty buck. I'd wanted to be an actress—not just an actress, because my heart's desire was to become a star like Jean Harlow. She was my dream of what I wanted, and that dream never let me be, even though I knew I'd never reach such a place."

With her hair bleached, mimicking Harlow's toughness and "snap," Grace became a "good time gal," a drinker, party girl, "boozing with the Hollywood second-grade movie crowd where you got a chance to rub elbows with the likes of what I'd wanted to become... That was the smart side, saying I better hold on to some security because the closest I'd get to a sound stage was cutting the film they were exposing."

The two fast became friends and before long were roommates, sharing an apartment east of Hollywood in the Silver Lake district, a five block walk from Consolidated.

Nothing stopped the parties: the two ran rampant from Big Bear to Huntington Beach, all night flappers and bootleg liquor flowing nonstop. "This was the Roaring Twenties," Grace would say. If you weren't living it up you were practically dead. The free sex of decades later had nothing over the twenties.

Gladys ran into Martin Mortensen, a meter-reader with the Los Angeles Gas & Electric Company, a self-appointed "good Joe" out for a good time on off hours. Gladys, blonde and slinky, could "hold her liquor like a trooper," except maybe she was a little lopsided when she married Mortensen. "I warned her it wasn't going to work," Grace said, "but she went ahead and hooked up with him anyway..."

The couple married at the home of a Presbyterian minister in North Hollywood, an autumn day in 1924, and as Baker had once expressed to his child bride, meter-man Mortensen promised Gladys he'd love and cherish her and never let her slip away.

But months later, the marriage slipped—as Gladys became involved with the dark-haired, handsome man in charge of the day shift at Consolidated. Stanley Gifford, brown-eyed with a trim mustache, a "ladies man," was being sued for divorce. His estranged wife accused him of drug addiction and associating "with women he worked with of low and dissolute character, often boasting of his sexual conquest..."

Green-eyed and storming over Gladys' attentions to Gifford, Mortensen accused her of having an affair. The wrangling continued until Gladys packed her bags and went back to sharing the good times with Grace—and with Gifford, calling herself Gladys Baker instead of Mortensen.

After pleading for her to return, wanting her back as she ignored him, Mortensen finally filed for divorce, charging desertion. Gladys kept ignoring him and the legal papers, spinning in the Hollywood party circuits, believing as soon as Gifford was free, he would marry her. But another slipping, another topsy-turvy of hopes, and the fling stayed open-ended. Gifford called it quits. He'd had enough of the skinny blonde.

The uncontested divorce was granted to Mortensen. As far as Gladys was concerned it was no loss to anyone, though shortly she discovered she was almost three months pregnant and didn't know who the father was. She went to Gifford. He turned her down, though offered her money.

Plenty of girls were getting abortions, some using coat hangers, but some were also dying from the home scrapings or the handiwork of fly-by-night quacks. Afraid and not knowing what to do, Gladys turned to her mother for help, but Della didn't know how she could help. Grainger was traveling on business to Southeast Asia, and she was going with him.

According to a would-be actress friend of Grace McKee, "Gladys really had no idea who the father was, though she knew it wasn't Martin (Mortensen). Gladys had always been ready for a wing-ding, but she said there was the possibility that Stanley Gifford was the baby's father but he had denied it, and there was no way to prove it…"

By the end of May 1926, Gladys was in and out of labor—false alarms at first until she was admitted to the charity ward of the Los Angeles General Hospital. At nine-thirty on the morning of June 1, Gladys gave birth to her third child, a girl. She said she didn't want the baby.

Norma Jeane and Della Hogan

Unwanted

Years later, Marilyn told actress Susan Strasberg, "I don't believe my mother ever really wanted me... That was situated in the back of her mind and no matter what happened it wasn't going to change ..."

Della urged Gladys to consider "arrangements" to place the baby for adoption. She had named the baby Norma Jeane Mortensen, entering Mortensen on the birth certificate as father—though knowing Norma Jeane couldn't have been Martin's child.

She should have left the father's name blank, Della told her, as the baby was conceived and born out of wedlock. Della said Gladys "let the other two go," and she now needed to consider what she was going to do with Norma Jeane.

Gladys said she couldn't think about what she had to do. She had to work and there was no one to take care of a baby. But she couldn't just "let her go..."

One thing seemed certain, Della said, that Gladys would have to place the baby with a decent family until she was able to make arrangements to raise the child—if that's what she was really inclined to do.

She didn't know whether she was or not. She hadn't been able to take care of the previous children, Della reminded her, in fact Gladys had told the hospital her two previous children were dead. Della suggested it would have been better had Norma Jeane been stillborn.

For a time, Grainger had expressed concern over Della's mental hygiene as well as her health. Her strength appeared to be deteriorating, especially her breathing. At times she said there was something wrong with the air. Grainger had found it difficult to reason with her. She seemed unable to participate in another's point of view or entertain ideas contrary to her own. Her thinking, he said, had become "brittle" and on occasion she had said people were spying on her.

Stunned by her mother's comment that it would have been easier if the baby had been born dead, Gladys said she couldn't pass the infant into some indefinite void without following the route herself. She said she'd jump off a bridge or in front of a train rather than sign the baby to an

orphanage and never see the child again.

An orphanage was where a misbegotten infant belonged, Della insisted, instead of being dragged through life a bastard and a disgrace. The unfortunate parent could then realize their mistake and "wash" their hands of the problem.

Gladys was sick, drained by the ordeal and the uncertainty, yet even though she did not know which man had fathered the baby, she wasn't going to surrender authority as the child's mother. Yes, she said, it would be necessary for the baby to be taken care of while she worked and tried to save money. Just so no one got the idea that she was giving away the baby forever. She would assume the role of mother later, not that of taking care of an infant, but happy to raise a smart young girl she'd never let go.

Della's neighbors, the good Christian people across the street, tended several foster children. She told Gladys she would have to pay for the care—a minimal sum since the state allotted a stipend to foster parents. She would ask if they would take a newborn baby as a foster charge.

Days later, baby Norma Jeane was delivered across the street to Albert and Ida Bolender. The religious couple detested booze, cigarettes, dancing and movies. They attended church regularly with their foster charges;

bible classes every week. "We live by the Word of God," Ida Bolender told Gladys.

Albert Bolender was a postman while Ida supplemented their income with the foster parenting. With newborn Norma Jeane in their care, Gladys returned to Hollywood, convincing herself she had made the right decision. She resumed work with Grace McKee, enjoying the life they had led before she became pregnant.

During the following year, Gladys made little contact with the Bolenders and rarely saw the baby. She's too young, Gladys would say. Time would come when the child would understand that Gladys was her mother.

The baby weighed on Grace McKee's mind. She had little first-hand knowledge of Gladys' marriage to Baker or the children she had surrendered to him. But she wondered, what was to become of the baby now boarded out to the Bolenders?

Marilyn had scant memories of her grandmother—vague shapes, shadows. The most vivid incident, recalled later as if a brief, hazy scene in a movie, was so overwhelming it imprinted itself in her mind like a brand. How Marilyn remembered and carried the picture is a mystery. I

have had to assume she was told of the occurrence, and repeated the brief story years later to Susan Strasberg, in whispered, stuttered syllables she stressed had to be kept secret.

The tale involved Della occasionally crossing the street to the Bolenders and asking to see the baby—Norma Jeane. One afternoon she said she believed the baby had died, and that no one was telling Della. Ida Bolender, perplexed and uneasy, assured Della the baby was fine. Della demanded to see the baby. Then, alone with Norma

Grace and Gladys with BeBe and Norma Jeane

Jeane, Della unsuccessfully tried to smother the baby with a pillow.

Ida Bolender grabbed the baby and Della said she was "trying to make it comfortable but the pillow had slipped on top of the baby…"

It would be difficult to determine if Ida grasped the situation completely—or knew what had happened, though she had her "suspicions" that the baby's grandmother was "an unhealthy person…"

For some time, Della had been ill and on medication, her moods and behavior extreme. They took a turn for the worse when she was notified that her father was dead. He had committed suicide by hanging himself from a rafter in the barn.

Della's illnesses grew worse. She often complained of losing her breath—of some kind of suffocation. She was suffering from a respiratory infection that was creating pressure on her heart. She accused people of plotting against her. She told Gladys she suspected the butcher at the market put fragments of glass in the meat grinder.

Meanwhile, across the street, the Bolenders provided Norma Jeane with an environment free of abuse and deprivation, their religious and domestic structures not so fundamental as to stifle the foster children.

Norma Jeane enjoyed a fairly "normal childhood," as psychiatrists would have it. It never occurred to her to question the identity of the Bolenders as her biological parents—a child, until reaching an age at which she can comprehend what parentage actually is, does not even consider those raising her as "parents." They are simply there, filling in the child's mind the assumed roles of mother and father.

Norma Jeane was no different in that respect, though later in life, Marilyn would ask, "Was it seven years? I don't know. It had to be seven years. I know I thought the Bolenders were my parents for a long time, and that the other children were related to me, though they did come and go. I didn't know until one day when I called Ida Bolender 'mom,' and was told she wasn't my mother. She said the lady that sometimes came to see me, 'the one with the red hair,' was my mother. I would see her so infrequently... And she never hugged me or kissed me. I never saw her smiling or laughing, but then she would tell me how happy I was going to be when we would be together, the two of us—and soon I would come away and be living with her. We would be so happy together. But she would say that to me and then she would...I never knew when she was coming back, or if she was coming back."

Marilyn said she had always thought of Mr. Bolender as her father. "I

was corrected by Mrs. Bolender and no one spoke about my father nor did they seem to know who he was. The Bolenders were sometimes strict and very religious. I was told so many things were bad and that people could not get into Heaven unless things were relinquished from their lives. I did not always believe in my heart that what I was told was true...There were so many other things in the world and I knew all of them could not be wrong...But what choice did I have? I did not know how to make such a choice. I guess I

Lester Bolender and Norma Jeane
Both Age 5
First boyfriend

felt as though I wasn't allowed to make choices because that was part of the things that were wrong..."

One afternoon Della crossed the street, "acting like she was in a rage," recalled Ida Bolender. "She was saying she believed the baby had died. She demanded to see the baby. By then Norma Jeane wasn't a small baby, and we were afraid to let her grandmother in. She was acting wildly and then she broke the glass of the front door. It was necessary to call the police."

That summer Della was delivered to Norwalk Mental Hospital,

The Bolenders and Norma Jeane

where her symptoms were described as "manic depressive psychosis." Nineteen days later she died from heart failure during a manic seizure which Gladys, and later Marilyn, came to believe as the stain of insanity that seemed to run rampant in the family.

Convinced that both her parents had died insane, Gladys now feared that she too would face the same fate. The thought began to weigh like an awful breath on her neck and her concerns centered on the little girl she had placed in another's care for seven years.

Her grandfather's suicide and the madness of her mother and father sent a sense of dread draining into her life. Gladys had to scramble—lose nothing further, retrieve the child she'd left with the Bolenders at her "insane" mother's urging.

Through associates at the Columbia film lab, Gladys gathered details of President Roosevelt's New Deal proposal –the Home Owner Loan Corporation, offering low-cost mortgages to thousands of Americans. Gladys, as a single mother, qualified and the purchase of a house was quickly initiated—a furnished, six-room, three bedroom house on Arbol Drive near the Hollywood Bowl. She got a loan from the Mortgage Guarantee Company of California, and Gladys and daughter moved into the house. Norma Jeane discovered a painted white, baby grand piano and asked happily, "Will this be our house forever?" Gladys said yes. This was the happiness Gladys had promised her—mother and daughter sharing a new life in the heart of Hollywood.

Norma Jeane and her mother would walk down Highland Avenue to Hollywood Boulevard, visit the shops and enjoy a chocolate sundae at C. C. Brown's down the boulevard from Grauman's Chinese Theatre. They would stroll to the Pig 'n Whistle, share a root beer float, then walk outside to the Egyptian Theatre. Other days they rode the streetcar to downtown L.A. Norma Jeane would see the lavish movie houses—"like palaces," she'd say. Often she dozed on the ride back to Hollywood, her head cradled against her mother's shoulder.

In their new home, Norma Jeane was learning to play the piano. She dreamed of someday sitting on a stage like in the Orpheum theatre downtown, a spotlight shining as she played the piano.

Grace McKee seemed to second Norma Jeane's daydreams, only presented a different scenario. Yes, there would be spotlights but a director would be beside a movie camera and he would say "Action!" and Norma Jeane would burst open like a big flower. Grace told her, you will be a fine actress, Norma Jeane—better than a fine actress, you will be a star—like Jean Harlow.

To insure Norma Jeane's well being, Gladys took out medical insurance and deposited money into a special account at the bank on Hollywood Boulevard at Highland Avenue. As Della had once done to guarantee security of the house, Gladys leased the house to an elderly British couple, the Atkinsons, renting two small rooms for themselves and sharing the living room, kitchen and bath with the couple. Norma Jeane was told they'd be sharing the house with other people.

On a visit to Gay's Lion Farm on Mission east of downtown L.A. with her mother and Grace, Norma Jeane became disturbed that the lions were trained to perform, "in ways," she'd say, "that were not natural for them if they had been left on their own...I was young but I had a thought that I would be kind of like an old, scrubby lion that was doing something it hadn't been intended on doing since it was born. And that thought scared me because I saw if I wasn't doing what I was supposed to be, then I would have had no idea what I was supposed to be doing since I was born."

The Atkinsons seemed an odd pair, pleasant enough with their "funny English accent," as Marilyn would recall. George Atkinson was a stand-in for actor George Arliss, who Grace spoke of often and had taken Marilyn to see in the movie, *The Green Goddess*. Atkinson also had a few bit parts in George Arliss pictures while his wife worked infrequently as an extra, and their daughter was stand-in for actress Madeleine Carroll.

Talk in the house on Arbol was usually of movies and movie business—of gossip and stars and Hollywood tales which Norma Jeane absorbed like a sponge. One afternoon Mr. Atkinson called her into the living room and held up a movie magazine with Joan Bennet on the cover. Atkinson announced that Norma Jeane looked like a young Joan Bennet. Norma Jeane blushed—she didn't think she looked like that, but Mrs. Atkinson  insisted there was a strong resemblance, especially in the eyes and the upper half of Norma Jeane's face.

Grace, her "mentor" said, "Well, there is a resemblance because you are both so pretty," but, no, she said proudly, the real resemblance Norma Jeane showed to another star was to Jean Harlow.

Another part-time movie stand-in and would-be actor was invited by the Atkinsons to stay at the house. The man took over a small back bedroom and kept grinning at Norma Jeane. She would remember this man watching her, smiling, or sometimes trying to tickle her. Once while she was playing the piano the man put his hand on her backside. He laughed, said he was "kidding" her, trying to surprise her.

Another time he gave her a hard chocolate bar which she didn't like. She told her mother "the man in back" had given it to her and Gladys replied, "That was nice of him. He is trying to be friendly."

Ida Bolender had warned the children never to accept gifts from strangers. Norma Jeane repeated this to her mother, but Gladys said the nice man wasn't a stranger. He was renting the room from the Atkinsons and they had the say-so about who would stay at the house.

Was the house no longer Norma Jeane's and her mother's? She wanted to know if the house was theirs, as her mother has told her so often—that it was their home—or did it belong to the Atkinsons?

Gladys told her she was too young to understand. It was their house but they had leased it to the Hollywood family.

The man offering candy was Mr. Kimmel—or Mr. Kinnel, or perhaps his name could have been Mr. Kenner. Marilyn would never be sure of the name, but whoever he was Norma Jeane would carry the scar from that particular afternoon.

The door to the small room was open and the man was wearing pajamas. He told her he had something for her and invited her into the room, saying something like, "After all, it's your mother's house, right?" Remembering that her mother had said it was okay, she stepped into the room. The man was looking for a sucker, he said, one he knew she would like. Norma Jeane didn't want it because it would be hard and she didn't like the taste. But she didn't say anything.

He shut the door. She would later remember the moment the door shut she felt something was wrong and her heart began to pound. "My heart was pounding so hard I couldn't breathe," she said. Something was going to happen because he was looking at her in a funny way, his face sweating, his lips raised above his teeth.

While he peeled the paper off the sucker, he told her to sit on his lap and they could visit. He'd tell her about the movies. She didn't want to get near him but he snatched her hand and drew her nearer. When he tried to get the sucker between her tightly pursed lips, some instinct to run seized her and she tried to jerk away. He kept holding her, pulling her towards him. She wanted to scream but she couldn't—she was afraid to scream but was so scared she felt she was going to scream. Then he put his hand over her mouth and pulled her against him.

The unbearable closeness made her dizzy and weak. If she got too dizzy she would not be able to get away. He was hurting her and she fought. She struggled, her small arms flying from his wet grasp. Kicking at him, she was able to break away and she ran for the door. He was right behind her.

Once out of the room she couldn't stop crying. Gladys wanted to know what was wrong. Norma Jeane was afraid to speak. What was wrong? Why was she so upset? Norma Jeane blurted out what had happened but wasn't able to finish because Gladys slapped her across the face. So stunning was the slap, Norma Jeane fell back. Gladys grabbed her and told her never to "say such a thing!" The man was a tenant—a nice man. Norma Jeane was bad for making up such a story.

Marilyn later would be convinced that at that moment her mother changed her life. A falling away of Norma Jeane's dreams of having a

house with her mother—the two of
them, Norma Jeane loved and cared for
by her mother. The dream collapsed
and she saw herself emptied from life—
cut off, punished and abandoned.

Years later, Marilyn would ask, "Do
you know what it's like to be forced into
uncertainty?"

The man who had done something
so wrong she couldn't shut it away was
never to be punished. Norma Jeane was
the one who'd been punished. The man
would pretend to be God-fearing and
pray for sinners but never, in Norma
Jeane's mind, would he turn that view
upon himself. The slap by Gladys set Norma Jeane against her mother.
She would never again feel deeply or yearn to be joined in a closeness with
Gladys Baker.

Choking back the truth, Norma Jeane felt now that Gladys was not her
mother. Later, she'd write, "I should have known that she is not really my
mother." She had no mother. No father. She was alone. No one would
listen to her, so she'd shut up. She'd keep her mouth shut.

Marilyn stuffed the incident into herself. It churned and muddled with
other pictures and tales she fabricated, weaving together her own understanding of the life she had led—shutting up, saying nothing, swallowing
the treachery visited upon her by the sweating man with the sucker, followed by her mother's lashing at her. The sting of that slap would stay as
long as she'd live. In time she'd concoct tales of other assaults against her,
or mistreatment and abandonment, reinventing the scene with the sweating stand-in over and over like a Movieola machine running full-tilt.

Sex was something to be looked at as ugly. Later she'd feel arousal
and the need for something but she couldn't allow into her life the same
thing that had happened in the back bedroom of the Arbol house. The incident festered into a sore that wouldn't heal. She didn't know how she
could keep on living with the way that it hurt.

As though a stake had been driven to separate their paths, daughter
wouldn't reach for the mother and the mother was slowly losing the ability to reach to the daughter. Gladys picked at food, stared at walls, sat for

hours without moving. She wasn't working. She was drinking again, on top of taking medication for depression. At times she would look at Norma Jeane and ask, "Who are you?" Norma Jeane would run from the room and hide in a closet.

Grace tried to fill the gap, to unite the mother and daughter in some way, but Gladys seemed to be drifting as if in a stream or a cloud. Trying to reach Gladys was like stirring the air, floating her further away. "You've got to buck up," Grace would say. "Norma Jeane needs you."

Marilyn later said, "She never needed me. She had no real attachments to me, and I imagine I wasn't even part of her memory." She recalled Grace asking her to kneel and join in a prayer to deliver good health to Gladys. Norma Jeane recited a prayer she'd learned from the Bolenders. Grace smiled, hugging Norma Jeane, reluctant to tell the girl she believed her depressed mother was having a nervous breakdown. It was a nightmare to consider that Norma Jeane's grandmother had lost her mind, and now Gladys was on the verge. It was too frightening to consider. Norma Jeane had been treated rotten—neglected. She had been unwanted, in the way. But Grace believed the girl could be safe from neglect and the harm that could befall her because of the complications suffered by Gladys.

One afternoon Gladys began raving—screaming and laughing hysterically. An ambulance had to be called and Gladys was taken away.

The man who had hurt Norma Jeane was gone. Only the Atkinsons were in the house, along with Norma Jeane, but the stand-ins were dis-

gruntled, dissatisfied. They planned on returning to England. Mr. Atkinson said Hollywood was "for cannibals..."

Believing she could reach Norma Jeane, Grace used soothing words, coaxing tones, thrown off at times as second thoughts reaching directly into Norma Jeane. She seemed to be saying that if the girl had not had the care and love she should've had, and if no one was willing to take her on as their own, Grace would.

She'd say to Norma Jeane, "I'm willing to set aside anything for you in seeing that you're happy and feeling that you've got a home—somewhere to belong and someone to care about you." But, she'd say, it was more than having a place to settle down and "kick off your shoes…" What Grace was talking about was a future, shiny as a diamond. She'd hold up a photograph of Jean Harlow. She didn't have to say anything. Marilyn said later, "She would be holding the picture and smiling and I'd look at it and smile, too, because I knew what she was showing me…" Norma Jeane could someday fill the kicked-off shoes of Jean Harlow.

Norma Jeane and friend Holly

"I know the qualities you have," Grace insisted. They were the same as Harlow. She could see Norma Jeanne's beauty and how she'd turn out when she outgrew the child, emerging as a young, beautiful woman. Grace was emphatic. Norma Jeane would be even more beautiful than Harlow, and that, she said, "has got to be a God-given miracle."

Norma Jeane drank in the words and proclamations as though gulping a glass of chocolate milk. Grace would whisper, "Doesn't that sound right? Don't you think being a star like Jean Harlow will make you feel good and proud?"

Norma Jeane spent a lot of time nodding. She also stuttered. Marilyn said, "Aunt Grace would say things to me like no one else would ever talk to me…She would sit me down and tell me things and hold my hands. I felt as whole as a loaf of bread nobody's ever eaten."

The only drawback to the thrilling predictions was that she'd have to wait until she grew up more in order to take her place in the same kind of movies she'd watch at the matinee. Giving her a "preview of coming attractions," Grace would skillfully apply makeup to Norma Jeane. She bought her white cotton gloves to wear whenever she was in public, and a wide-brimmed hat to shade the skin of her precious face from the scorching summer sun.

"There…" Grace would say confidently, appraising the results of her cosmetic skills. "You are going to be a star, Norma Jeane, and the world will love you."

It was 1934, Norma Jeane was eight and on occasion accompanied Grace to the studio where she paraded her as the "next Jean Harlow." Grace seemed to be claiming the girl as her personal discovery, but the shy Norma Jeane was embarrassed, uncomfortable by the encouraged attention.

They would lunch at the commissary where Norma Jeane might see "real live" movie stars face to face.

Ernest Neilson knew Grace from Consolidated. "She was a sparkling lady in many ways," he says. "What you call a gem of a human being. Her energy and cheerfulness bubbled at you, and her laugh was contagious, so even if you didn't know what you were laughing about, you were still laughing. I remember when she brought Norma Jeane to the lab— a real treat for the girl who was very ladylike, even then, like a small lady in a wide-brimmed sun hat and all made-up to look glamorous.

"Grace announced that she was grooming the girl to be the next Jean Harlow...I suppose she was obsessed about it or like a ritualized pastime, turning the kid into thinking she would be a star like Harlow. When I first met Norma Jeane, the girl curtsied, so of course I took her hand and gave it a little kiss because she was so primped like a little princess. To me it was like a horse in training to run the races, but we got a wallop of a surprise years later when that actually became a fact—the girl became a movie star.

"I keep remembering that curtsy, a little like Shirley Temple or Miss Muffet...Something you saw in a movie even back then. She'd greet you with saying, 'How very pleased I am to make your acquaintance,' and then before you said anything, she'd say, 'My name is Norma Jeane and I'm going to be a star!' That caught you straight off, then Grace right behind her, nudging her ahead with a smile as proud as a chicken's mother."

Sometimes on weekends Grace would take Norma Jeane on the trolley down Hollywood Boulevard. They would get off at Vine Street to stroll the length of the boulevard to Grauman's Chinese Theatre. "Paying respects," Grace put it, and they'd touch Jean Harlow's hand and footprints in the concrete, surrounded by all the other great stars' inscriptions.

Grace would tell Norma Jeane stories about Mary Pickford and Douglas Fairbanks, about Charlie Chaplin and Fay Wray. They would attend the old movies and Norma Jeane's eyes would glow. Later at home she'd hold the same glow—scenes from movies rolling through her head.

Grace was always there at her shoulder. "Someday you will be at Grauman's Chinese," she'd tell Norma Jeane, "and it will be you putting your handprints and footprints in the cement. Do you know that? Can you believe that in the way that I can see that happening?"

After some time in the rest home, Gladys was released on weekends. She sat, a stranger to her daughter and to Grace. She seemed to have crept into some dark, solitary world and shut an impenetrable door. Grace tried to tell Norma Jeane that her mother could be getting better but neither believed the story. If anything, Gladys was getting worse.

She was transferred to Los Angeles General Hospital where she was diagnosed as insane. Grace told Norma Jeane, "Your mother might not be coming home so we will have to make plans..." Marilyn would later tell John Stix in New York, "My mother never wanted to be my mother and then she turned against me. She went insane when my grandfather hanged himself. My mother and I were together only a very short time and then that was the end..."

Grace tried to adopt Norma Jeane but was notified by the state that proof of the incompetence of the biological parents was required. Meanwhile, Norma Jeane cut pictures from movie magazines Grace bought her, along with the photographs of stars pilfered from the studio lab. She bought Norma Jeane a scrapbook with a brown cardboard cover and took the initiative at pasting in the cutouts and photos—crowding the scrapbook pages with images of the stars who had pressed their prints into wet concrete at Grauman's. Grace told Norma Jeane, "Some day, honey, a whole bunch of girls will be filling their own scrapbooks with pictures of you because they'll be dreaming of becoming stars just like you're going to be."

As they spent hours in the lavish movie palaces along Broadway, Grace would be drinking in the lives lived on the screen while Norma Jeane stayed enraptured at her side. Some days they'd have a fancy brunch—not every weekend but occasionally "a special treat," and Grace was quick to say that some day Norma Jeane would have the same brunches as a matter of course.

"It was like learning a trade or how to navigate a boat," Marilyn recalled. "I honestly felt that all the things I learned from Grace were the same as being delivered to myself. I was afraid not to believe her because there wasn't anything else I could believe in, except what I wanted, and that was a home with someone who would love me...Of course I didn't say that to anyone..."

Neilson says there seemed more to Grace's desires to create in the girl a replica of Harlow. She was instilling in Norma Jeane what Grace herself had longed for in muted desperation — the fame and adulation she sensed was hopelessly beyond her reach. Norma Jeane would someday do it, Grace said again and again.

"She was the closest person in my life," Marilyn said. "I can't say if I was the closest to her because I felt, you know, she believed in my becoming something I wasn't at the time. So it was all make-believe. Possibly my wanting to be with her was like more schooling, and there was the teacher and a student. Grace wanted that relationship like she had found herself in me or what she believed I could become..."

The stand-ins were gone and the Arbol house was going into receivership.

Grace had been able to secure a statement from the hospital that Gladys Baker was insane, and her minor daughter had been illegitimate. By January, 1935, Grace had succeeded in having Gladys transferred from Los Angeles General Hospital's psychiatric ward to the Norwalk State Hospital — the same institution where Della had died.

Marilyn would later say, "What I was told was right always turned out to be wrong, and it brought a sadness you aren't sure why you're feeling, as though someone so very close has passed away. I believed my mother wasn't in the world anymore. The sadness I felt stayed with me all the time." She described the feeling as if hearing footsteps behind her on an otherwise empty street. "No one is there," she said. "The same as a shadow that is attached to your own shadow, you know, and it is not your own."

57

From General Hospital to RKO

I think the charity section of L.A. General Hospital where Marilyn was born became a psycho ward before it was torn down. The current concrete monolith went up the same year L.A.'s City Hall thrust skyward in a deco needle like a bullet aimed at heaven. My father was working a Depression job linked to constructing the central library—a kind of mystic hybrid of Masonry and metaphysics, still a treasure of the city of angels. So much of the past as laid out in bricks, boards and cement has been erased by dynamite or shovels, flattened for freeways and parking lots or birthed into what they could've called skyscrapers back in the days when an earthquake summoned the city's boogey man.

They said they had the quake-phobia licked, and all these movie-set colossi would do is jiggle around the fault line like a row of those rubber hula dancers on your dashboard.

In 1935, when I was born in L.A. General Hospital, Marilyn was still Norma Jeane, nine years ahead of me. My grandmother who raised me and Marilyn's mother who didn't raise her knew Depression Los Angeles like nobody knows it now. Then later, the war and the ration books, the gas pinches, the studio strikes, the pickets and breakers while folks in Detroit and Indiana or down in Texas dreamed of an L.A of milk and honey where you'd open your window and pluck an orange swaying in a sea breeze beneath a bright blue sky.

I was born a pretty baby—a face fitted onto me that I'd later be tyrannized by. Marilyn somehow propelled from way back to stand in the limelight while I'd bust, disabled at getting a wholeness across as I funneled myself into a role, that heat bottling in me as I felt the fire stoking yet couldn't find the exit.

We were both raised around Hollywood, and both in the Valley. My step-grandfather worked as head carpenter for RKO Radio Pictures and had built the sets for *Swiss Family Robinson*, starring Thomas Mitchell, Edna Bret, Freddie Bartholomew and Tim Holt. I'd been on the lot as a kid, same as Marilyn had, and was no doubt no less mystified seeing in the flesh the faces we'd view on the matinee screens.

59

Separately, we had saved nickels. I kept my secret stash of buffalos and pennies in a White Owl cigar box. Marilyn later told me she'd hide her nickels in a shoe she hated— too big and flat like a duck's foot or a kind of pancake.

Originally from Belfast, my grandmother was a soft touch for the Irish. She housed a

"Aunt" Ana and Norma Jeane

perpetual boarder named Jack McCormick, a movie extra and Merchant Marine working a Matson Line steamship operating from L.A Harbor to Honolulu and back. He'd tell me about the sailors and soldiers double-lined around the Hotel Street whorehouses.

Marilyn's first husband, who'd be twenty-two when he married the sixteen year old Norma Jeane, became a Merchant Marine and later a Los Angeles policeman.

My father was an L.A. cop, divorced from my mother. She'd been a bit player at MGM studios, a drinking pal of Jean Harlow and friends with Richard Arlen and John Darrow who had co-starred with Harlow in Howard Hughes' *Hell's Angels*. Darrow later became my agent when I lurched from kid actor into younger leading man on the verge of being groomed for stardom.

As a kid, Marilyn spent time on the studio lots where she'd dream of waltzing through the sound stages as another Jean Harlow. Before long she'd emerge from an imposed cocoon as the world's most beautiful and vital movie star, eclipsing even Harlow. But through the joy of bright achievement that was to come, there clung to Marilyn a kind of shadow few could see, an unshakable cloud. She was a sad and strange girl—diffident yet glowing and vivacious, determined yet fearful and timid as a gazelle.

Before that rainbow crested, Marilyn and I ran separately in and out of Hollywood's glass bubble. She was nine years ahead of me, but in a short spell we caught up in the industry—the same people hitting the same spots from Sunset Strip's Mocambo to the Coconut Grove and Miracle Mile.

Wynn Rocamora was my first agent, then Johnny Darrow, but not before Henry Willson had me on kid dates with Natalie Wood. We'd be sucking separate straws from the same root-beer float in the now long-gone Pantage's Theatre snack bar at Hollywood and Vine. Or walking hand in hand along the pier in Santa Monica.

By 1935, Marilyn's mom was lodged into Patton State Hospital. While I was still on the baby bottle, not knowing I'd be bounced out by my mom and dad's divorce, Marilyn was being plucked from the house by the Hollywood Bowl, weeping over the loss of the white piano, and left in a stranger's apartment on Lodi Place in Hollywood.

Grace, her sworn guardian, was making sure the girl had a roof above her while what belonged to Gladys was being disposed of. Bills were being paid and the world Norma Jeane had wanted so desperately to be a happy one had turned to ash. Then something unexpected happened during the disbursement of the property. Grace met a would-be actor. He was ten years younger than Grace, a divorced man with three kids living in Las Vegas. "It was like the song," Grace said later, "one of those things that just happens. I hadn't planned on it or wanted to get involved but there it was..."

She married Ervin Goddard in Las Vegas, Nevada, and one of the Goddard children, Nona, returned to Los Angeles with the newlyweds. They rented a small house in Van Nuys, over the hill from Hollywood, then Grace quickly packed up Norma Jeane, "plucked out of somewhere else once again," and brought her to live with them. Grace told her, "You've become a member of the family. This will be your new home and I will take care of you, Norma Jeane. You even have a step-sister now..."

Nona would later say, "Norma Jeane was a shy, introverted girl, but we were both neurotic kids and tended to keep our mouths shut around the grownups... We were very secretive. We had a tree house and we'd climb up into it and hide when we thought we were going to get into trouble. That was our escape...I was just little back then and Norma Jeane was older than me but I felt like she was really my big sister..."

A few times, Norma Jeane would retreat to the little tree house even without Nona, who would be sent to bring Norma Jeane back into the house.

Earnings were thin and a short time later Goddard decided that Norma Jeane was "just one more mouth" than they could afford to feed. He told Grace repeatedly, "It's not like she's your own daughter, not like Nona is my daughter, and we

can't afford to support her right now." He said the best thing for "all concerned" would be to send Norma Jeane to an orphanage. He'd thought it over, he said. "She needs to live someplace else until things improve financially."

Reluctantly, Grace sent Nona to find Norma Jeane, then took her for a short walk. She told her she would have to go to an orphanage "for a little while—"

Why? Why? Norma Jeane cried. She begged to know why she had to go away. Grace tried to explain that it had to do with the lack of money, but there was no real answer for Norma Jeane. Another broken life. Another "mother" turning against her—another "mother" deserting her. Norma Jeane realized in some way that each event in her life was proving that she could be gotten rid of easily when it was no longer con-venient for her to be where she was.

She had no say in the matter. She clammed up, watching Grace pack her few possessions into a small suitcase and a shopping bag, including a handful of seashells Norma Jean had gathered and placed on a windowsill "so the sun would shine on them because they were pret-ty..." Norma Jeane cried as they drove over the hill to the Orphanage Home in Hollywood. It would be all right, Grace kept saying. Everything would change very soon.

Marilyn said, "I thought I was going to a prison. What had I done, that they were getting rid of me? I was afraid of everything and afraid to show how scared I was and all I could do was cry."

Grace and an attendant had to pull Norma Jeane from the car.

Not all of the fifty or so kids at the orphanage were orphans. Some, in the same boat as Norma Jeane, were called "unwanted children," young ones who'd been in the way and set on the shelf "for the time being."

From that September of '35 until her eleventh birthday in 1937, Norma Jeane remained at the orphanage. Years later, her recollections of life at the orphanage became more and more fantastic. Tales of dark rooms and drudgery, of "forced labor—" nights cleaning toilets or scrubbing floors and washing dishes until her knuckles and knees bled. The stories were false, memories fabricated in a kid's mind like scabs covering real abrasions—the terror of being unwanted, rejected by all and as expendable as a paper doll. Thrown away by her mother before she was two weeks old, made promises to and cheated out of anything good happening to her. Packed up like trash in a shopping bag and stuck somewhere where all her volition was stripped away. Norma Jeane had no one, and nobody loved Norma Jeane.

Years later, Marilyn told Ralph Roberts, "When I was ten years old I used to wake up sometimes and I'd think I was dead, like I had died in my sleep, and I wasn't part of my body anymore. I couldn't feel myself and I thought could it be that the world has ended? Everything seemed so far away and like nothing else could bother me..."

Days she attended Vine Street Elementary School, a five minute walk from the orphanage. Sometimes a visit from Grace on a Saturday. She would take Norma Jeane for an outing and maybe have lunch in a restaurant along Hollywood Boulevard. Maybe they would see a movie—Jean Harlow and Clark Gable in *China Seas* or Harlow in *Libeled Lady*. One day, a very special day, Grace brought Norma Jeane a white dress. "White is the color for you." Norma Jeane thought Grace was taking her out of the orphanage, but Grace said no, she was arranging for Norma Jeane to attend a movie premier to see the stars.

Again they visited Grauman's Chinese to see the handprints, the footprints and the inscriptions, Norma Jeane again fitting her hands in Jean Harlow's prints. Her feet were bigger than Harlow's. Grace said "Jean had tiny feet like some of those Chinese girls, only Jean's size was determined by God and so many of those Chinese girls were forced to look that way, and certainly not by God."

Grace took her to a beauty parlor on Sunset and had Norma Jeane's hair curled. Makeup was applied to her face—lipstick and rouge like a grown-up lady. A picture was taken of Norma Jeane and Grace called

her a "China doll." Studying the nine year old, Grace assured her she would someday be a famous movie star and *every*body would love her. She said, "You look just like Jean Harlow when she was a little girl."

But where will I live? Norma Jeane asked. Who will be with me? Why, anywhere she wanted to live, Grace told her, as long as it wasn't far from the studio where Norma Jeane would be making movies. Taking Norma Jeane's hand, Grace said, "Everybody will want to be with you. Things will be different in a short time, honey. You will see."

From this abandonment, her sense of self nose-dived straight to the dirt, not that it had ever gotten too far off the ground. Her sense of worth and esteem would never climb above her role of rejectee.

Marilyn would describe the world she'd been "dumped" into as "grim," enclosing her in a cold, *grim* environment she'd remember all her life. The only comfort she knew was in pretending she wasn't where she was. She could make up another world for herself. She could live in that make-believe place instead of "drowning or suffocating" in what she'd been forced to endure. The world in the movies and magazines was closed to Norma Jeane. She was on the outside with no longer a way of looking into their world, only into her own "secret place..."

She cried at nights, her face muffled with a blanket so nobody'd yell at her. Outside her window she could see the water tower sticking up from the studio lot at RKO Radio Pictures. She wondered if she'd be crying so hard and so long her tears could fill that water barrel.

Traitorous was a Word

Norma Jeane learned the word *traitorous* at the elementary school she'd walk to and from while housed at the orphanage. A traitor could not be trusted. Traitors were people who betrayed those who were close to them—those who had believed in them.

Sometimes she'd shut her eyes and imagine strolling through a field of flowers while holding hands with her mother and a father—"a man who looked like Clark Gable." She could trust that person.

The length of time she spent in the Los Angeles orphanage remains inexact—whether close to a year or closer to two years, for Norma Jeane it seemed the length of a child's life. From time to time Grace would visit her, always with some small treat or a stroll through Hollywood.

In May of '37, Grace bought Norma Jeane a *Life* magazine that had Jean Harlow's picture on the cover. "I kept the picture at all times," Marilyn said later. "I wanted to frame the magazine cover, and then only a month later Jean Harlow died... "

The star was only twenty-six at the time of her death on June 7th. When Norma Jeane was officially "signed out" of the orphanage, she experienced a "strange" feeling of being "set free into a world in which Jean Harlow no longer lived."

She returned to the Goddard house, believing her life with Grace was secured now, but there was something ominous present. Ervin Goddard, now drinking heavily, was looking at Norma Jeane with the same glazed, "sneaky" expression as the sweaty stand-in had stared at her in the house she'd shared with her mother. Norma Jeane tried to stay away from Goddard. "A couple of times he said, 'Aren't you going to give me a kiss?' I would sneak out of the room..." she said. "He scared me..."

One night Goddard cornered her. She would never forget the sour smell of the liquor. He grabbed her and put his hands on her, fondling her, trying to reach between her legs as he forced himself on her. Norma Jeane broke from his grasp and ran crying—terrified, shaking—"my heart beating so fast I thought I would die."

She hid behind the garage until Grace returned, then quickly told her what had happened, saying she was "scared" to go back into the house.

Grace felt her stomach hit rock bottom. She believed some warnings had been broadcast way back when Goddard had insisted Norma Jeane be sent to an orphanage. Had he been trying to remove the temptation? Was something

Grace McKee married Ervin Goddard, who sexually assaulted Norma Jeane

happening with his own seven year old daughter, Nona?

Goddard claimed the incident with Norma Jeane was nothing but a moment of "too much grog" and being "too playful with the kid—fooling around tickling her." He denied any "unhealthy" overtones to his actions. With a sickening feeling, Grace was aware of something beyond his casual explanation. She suspected the worst but the options were few. Would she leave her husband? Divorce him? Or would she— *could* she send Norma Jeane away again?

Her husband could change, she reasoned. Grace could stand him but not enough so that Norma Jeane could continue living with them. The girl was young with a life yet ahead of her. She could patch the gaps—the holes. Grace didn't have a life ahead of her. She was using it up.

Immediate plans were made and the next day Norma Jeane was shipped two dozen miles south to the city of Compton to stay with cousins—offspring of her mother's brother, Marion Monroe, a man who had strangely wandered off one evening and disappeared. The family was having him officially declared dead so finances could be forthcoming.

Money—whenever available—would be paid by Grace to the Monroes for Norma Jeane's care. In time, little was paid and the care was minimal.

Marilyn later said, "I can best describe that period as being in squalor. The other kids knew I was related to them, but I felt on a desert island with natives or primitive people out of the hills of Appalachia... I was more alone and separated from anything than I had ever been. I would awake and wouldn't know where I was. Was I still at the orphanage? It was dawning on me that I was feeling the predicament of my life, and that frightened and depressed me so much I would get sick and couldn't eat... When I did I would often throw up because my stomach could not hold the food. I could not even keep down orange juice or chicken noodle soup..."

For nine months Norma Jeane shared a bed with a cousin, Ida Martin. After what seemed like years on Devil's Island, other arrangements were made by Grace for Norma Jeane to stay in Hollywood with Grace's elderly aunt, Ana Lower.

Although "rejectee" could've been a second middle name for Norma Jeane, she'd usually been able to get along with other children. Turning teenager, things changed and she soon found herself the outcast—an oddball in every social setting. Her clothes were "dumb," the kids said. "She had no taste," one girl says. "She wore things that didn't match like it didn't even occur to her how she should look. Like you put together one half of somebody and the second half of somebody else. That's what she looked like."

Another says Norma Jeane was "jumpy and loud," looked like a "hick," and didn't know how to "get along" with anyone. "She didn't have any friends."

Barbara Long, fourteen at the time, says, "She didn't comb her hair very well and she didn't wear any makeup like some girls did. She wasn't liked by any of the other girls and right away was ostracized and picked on. It wasn't fair. She got a bad reputation, and some of the boys—the more rowdy ones—believed she didn't show any class and so she had to be putting out. They'd go after her but she surely puzzled them because she was a wallflower. So for a while they called her an 'untouchable.' Norma Jeane the untouchable. She wouldn't get near anyone, but more like *she* was afraid everyone else had a disease and she might catch it. She was at a dance that year but I don't think she knew what to do or didn't want to do anything, though she *could* dance, but more like she wanted to go play ping-pong instead. So that only increased her bad reputation, kids thinking she was a snob on top of it. One time somebody threw a head of lettuce at her and she cried... There wasn't any way to get to know her."

Her "reputation" wasn't as bad as it was lacking. Another girl says, "Norma Jeane never struck you as a smart girl. If anything, you would have thought she was dumb because she didn't have anything going and just hung there—*hung* there like waiting for someone to take her off the wall and do something with her."

A boy named Bob dated her. "She had a portable radio," he recalls, "a Sears Silvertone portable that wasn't working and I fixed it for her. We went to the movies. She always wanted to go to the movies or talk about the movies. We'd eat popcorn and stuff or candy she always had from the old lady she was living with who wasn't her mother. She called her 'aunt' but I was told she wasn't her aunt which was weird, and that was more stuff for people to talk about.

"Maybe I'd get my arm around her and she didn't mind that but she didn't want to kiss or make out, and she wanted to talk instead—about the movies. Or she always was listening to that portable radio.

"We'd joke around a little and listen to songs and she liked to sing but she'd get sad and then just wouldn't say anything. Maybe she had reasons I didn't know about, but I didn't go out with her any more because I started going steady with someone else. Norma Jeane said to me once, 'I thought you were *my* friend!' Then she didn't seem to think it was too weird her wanting to go out with the girl and myself—like the three of us, and go to the movies or something. When I said we couldn't do that, she didn't seem to care, and seemed like she never even knew me... had no investment in our going around together like we had. We'd filled spare time... I never got close to *any*thing happening between us, and getting inside the scene, you know, Norma Jeane had that '*untouchable*' label stuck on her and no matter what anyone says, it stuck...

"The fact that *this* kid became *Marilyn Monroe* is an almost unbelievable, fantastic phenomenon that nobody even on the planet Mars would believe!"

Aunt Ana gave Norma Jeane a "big old teddy bear" that had a button for a nose, one blue eye and the other patched with a green button. "I slept with it every night," Marilyn told John Stix. "I can do a sense memory exercise about that bear in five seconds. I can feel it, I can smell it, I can hear it talking tome which is what I used to pretend almost every night."

"What did the teddy bear say to you?" John asked.

"It said, 'I love you, Norma Jeane...' There wasn't anybody around to say I was getting too big to sleep with a teddy bear, and I used to whisper to him that someday we'd have our very own home and we'd sleep in the same bed every night and not have to go to different beds all the time...

"My childhood was an extension of other people's expectations. I never had any control over what I was going to do or what was going to happen to me. I was alive except I didn't have a future, so it was like I wasn't really alive after all. I lived only in the moment and going from here to there with other people telling me where I'd go."

The Goddards were leaving California. Ervin Goddard had the opportunity of a job transfer and they would relocate to West Virginia. Norma Jeane was still a ward of the state and could not leave California.

Without the assistance of Grace, her Aunt Lower couldn't take care of Norma Jeane. Ana was suffering from heart trouble and unable to supervise the girl on a permanent basis, though it had seemed fairly permanent to Norma Jeane. She would later say it was the only time in her life that she felt loved, and had some sense of belonging.

Since she was only going on sixteen, Norma Jeane would have to go back to the orphanage, remaining there until she was eighteen. She said nothing. She wouldn't return to the orphanage. She'd run away—she would not go back. Nor could she be in the company of Ervin Goddard, even if it came to be that she was separated legally from California.

Always resourceful, Grace spoke to her neighbor, Ethel Dougherty. The neighbor had a son, Jim, then twenty-one, working for Lockheed Aircraft. Jim knew Norma Jeane. He had driven her in his car, taking her on errands, and once he drove her to a dance. Grace's casual suggestion

to Ethel Dougherty was presented as a wonderful solution to keeping Norma Jeane from being returned to the orphanage. She said, "I believe Jim has had a crush on her for a long time, and wouldn't it be nice if they got married?"

Taken by surprise, Ethel Dougherty said, "Well, Norma Jeane is a lovely girl. She's pretty and I'm sure Jim might be happy to consider taking her as his wife. But she's so young..."

Jim Dougherty said he'd marry her. He was planning on going into the Merchant Marines, and Norma Jeane would have a home with Ethel. He said to Norma Jeane, "I guess we're supposed to get married." She said yes. He said, "We should go buy a ring."

Norma Jeane said, "I don't know anything about being married."

"I don't either," Jim said. "I've never been married and I wasn't planning on it right now, actually..."

The marriage was arranged and Norma Jeane, just turned sixteen, told Grace, "I don't know anything about being married but I will do it..." She told Nona Goddard, who was then twelve, "I'll have my own house to live in and it will be like in the movies. I guess I have to learn how to cook something... I like tamales. Maybe he will like tamales."

On June 19, 1942, Jim Dougherty and Norma Jeane became man and wife. "We had a wonderful reception at a fancy place," Marilyn said, "and from that point on it was all down hill..."

Baring Skin

A Los Angeles cop friend of Jim Dougherty said the fanciful tales Dougherty bragged about as his happy times with the girl who became Marilyn "just wasn't the way he was actually living it..."

From the start of the marriage, Marilyn said she didn't want to have him doing something to her that was going to hurt. "She'd never had sex," the cop said, "which wasn't unusual back then and a guy liked the idea that his wife hadn't slept around. But with Dougherty, at first it was like she'd wanted to draw a boundary line that nobody was going to cross, even if he was her husband..."

Jim knew it was a matter of time before he was out of the country. "Once in the Merchant Marines," the cop said, "they went to Catalina where he underwent training and Norma Jeane wandered the town in a bathing suit that left almost nothing to your imagination. Sixteen years old with a body to bust a bomb. He wanted her wearing slacks or keeping herself covered. She wanted a suntan. He said lay in the yard where they were...

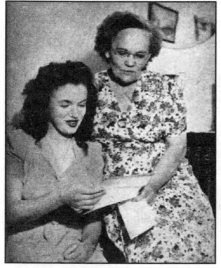

Norma Jeane and Mrs. Dougherty

"He didn't like her being looked at by other guys. She didn't seem to mind. Their bedroom behavior had improved a little, but she was always saying she was sick. When it came time to perform, she'd run around the place dusting with a feather duster and an apron and trying to make like she was doing something constructive as a wife, but all she was succeeding at doing was getting Jim hornier every day. He liked to go grab beers with his buddies and he said on a couple of occasions he took advantage of another female

75

and swore he'd never told a soul that. But since he liked to brag I don't know if he told anyone else or not. The only thing I know is they weren't comfortable in that department, and weren't very compatible in other ways."

While Dougherty was overseas, Norma Jeane lived with Jim's mother who taught her to drive, then got her a job in the Radio Plane Company, owned by the actor Reginald Denny. Apart from the Burbank operation, Denny also owned a popular model airplane hobby store in Hollywood. Norma Jeane's ten-hour day was spent spraying varnish on the fuselage fabric of small, no-pilot aircraft manufactured for target and antiaircraft training.

She wrote letters to Grace Goddard, living in West Virginia, telling of the happiness she shared with Jim in their marriage. This was not a fact but a rosy picture to please Grace—the matchmaker, a part of Marilyn's pretend games to bring forth approval.

One day several photographers from the U.S. Army's First Picture

Jim Dougherty and Norma Jeane at
The Coconut Grove

Unit arrived at the plant to take pictures of women working on the "home front," contributing to the war effort.

A few days after her seventeenth birthday, Norma Jeane wrote to Grace that she had been singled out by the army photographers. "They took a lot of moving pic-

76

tures of me," she wrote, "and some of them asked for dates, etc., (Naturally I refused!)... An army corporal by the name of David Conover told me he would be interested in getting some color shots of me. He used to have a studio on 'the Strip' on Sunset (Boulevard)... He is awfully nice and is married, and it is strictly business, which is the way I like it..."

Things changed fast. "Modeling for those pictures is what did it," Dougherty said later. "All those guys chasing after her, taking pictures of her. I wanted her to be a wife. I wanted to have kids—raise a family. I wanted a normal life. She didn't. She was after something that had nothing to do with the way normal people live their lives."

Potter Hueth, another photographer and friend of David Conover, met Norma Jeane through Conover after the two returned from a photo shoot in the desert. Conover told Hueth they had stayed at the Furnace Creek Inn in Death Valley, and he grinned, indicating he'd had "a marvelous time..."

Impressed with Conover's photos, Hueth invited Norma Jeane for a shoot. He had her posing in tight sweaters, or against a bale of hay, looking like a farm girl, and even shots with a Dalmatian. He told her he wanted her to meet a lady who ran a modeling agency in the Ambassador Hotel.

Hueth then took his photos of Marilyn to Emmiline Snively at the Blue Book agency. Miss Snively saw Norma Jeane's enormous potential and immediately arranged to have her trained and sent on assignments.

Snively urged Marilyn to lighten her hair. "Too dark," she said. "You need highlights and brightness so you'll stand out in the color shots."

She told Marilyn to go to Frank and Joseph's salon on Wilshire near the Ambassador. She told Marilyn, "You be sure, Norma Jeane, to see Sylvia Barnhart." She said she'd call Sylvia and let her know what they were looking for.

Sylvia Barnhart, a

slim, attractive young woman with arresting, exotic eyes, waited an hour and half past the time of the appointment. "I had no idea then who Norma Jeane was," says Sylvia, "and I wondered where she was and if there was a problem. I called the Blue Book but was told the girl had left to go across the street a little after two that afternoon. It was almost four."

No sooner had Sylvia hung up the phone when Marilyn strolled into the salon. She looked at Sylvia and said, "You must be Miss Barnhart..."

"I am," Sylvia said, "and you're two hours late for the appointment."

Marilyn said, "I am?" She looked frightened. "What should I do?"

"The girl was almost in tears," Sylvia says. With a sigh, she said, "Follow me, honey, and we'll get started." Sylvia says, "I never knew why it took her almost two hours to get across the street. It seemed crazy. She said she wasn't sure what had happened, but confessed she did have a kind of problem in sometimes being late— some sort of distractions. "*Some*times?"

With Sylvia Barnhart at Hair Show

Sylvia says. "The girl was *always* late. You could set your watch or place winning bets on her never showing up on time for anything. By late I mean she was consistently two *hours* late."

During that first appointment, Marilyn told Sylvia, "You're the first person that has ever really done something to my hair..." She said, "I know it must be a mess."

Her hair was a mess, says Sylvia. "Very kinky and drab—a drab

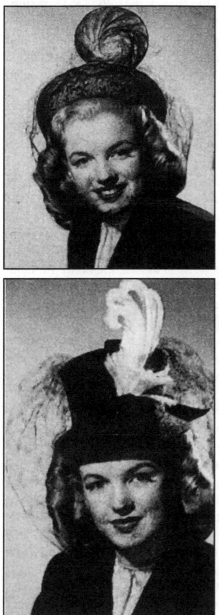

brown I won't even mention what the color was like, but it was all frizzy and kinky, and the agency had requested I turn her into a red-head. That's what they wanted— that's what they'd get."

Eyeing the photographs of movie stars on the salon wall, Marilyn asked Sylvia if she had worked with the stars. Sylvia said, "Yes, I have."

Marilyn said, "Well, some day I'll be a star and you're going to be my hairdresser."

"Is that what's going to happen?" Sylvia said. She says, "Norma Jeane nodded and I said, 'Hold your head still...' We worked and after a while she looked at me very seriously and said, 'I know I'm going to be a movie star.' She was serious. I said, 'Well, Norma Jeane, if you really believe that and if the fates are in your favor, then you very well might become what you've set your heart to be."

That was the beginning of a relationship between Marilyn and Sylvia that would last many years. "She was thrilled," Sylvia says, "as excited as a child to see her hair getting lighter and lighter, the kinkiness leaving. She had rich, lovely hair. Strong, with a luxurious texture. The girl was transforming in front of my eyes."

Marilyn's hair went from the "drab brown" to a lighter shade, appearing almost red at first. Photographer Bob Shannon told me, "I took shots of a couple girls working out of the agency in Hollywood one summer. Barbara Lawrence was working as a model, and later was doing movie work at Fox studios. Another girl I shot was Karen Weston and then Norma Jeane. When the sun was on her, her hair was almost like a lot of glowing rubies. I did shots of her and sold them before I relocated to Baltimore and got into publishing."

Shannon bought Norma Jeane a hotdog and she started to cry. "She got flushed in the face," he says, "tears in her eyes as if she was choking. I asked what was wrong and she painfully said she had a bad stomach ache...

"We didn't call off the shoot," he says, "I went to a drugstore and got a tin of aspirin she'd asked for, and then she took about five or so, and I said that was a lot of aspirin. Was that wise? She said it was okay. The only thing to kill the pain. I said that could kill the rest of you as well. She said it was severe 'monthly troubles,' and was embarrassed.

"She was married and he was overseas in the Merchant Marines, but she said she was going to be getting a divorce because he didn't appreciate that she was trying to build a career as a model. She'd been living with her mother-in-law, the guy's old lady, but she'd moved out of the house. She said she had nothing in common with her husband and there had never been any romance. She went on to say she had not had any real romance in her life and as it was she wasn't interested in romance. I asked her why she married the guy and she said it was an arrangement.

"Had she been pregnant?" I asked. She said she was never pregnant. It was an arranged marriage, she told me. I said like a family kind of thing? Yeah, that's what she'd meant. But she wanted to be in the movies—wanted to act in pictures, and I asked if she'd done any acting. She said she hadn't but wanted to study hard and learn how to do it. She was sure she could though she'd never done it."

Shannon claimed she was exceptional as a model, with a girl-next-door look and the sexy farmer's daughter all wrapped into one, plus a glamorous quality—"an American Dream Girl," he says, meaning she wasn't a vamp but had that homespun look and yet was very appealing—in a sexy way. But she said her mother-in-law didn't like what she was doing, didn't approve of a young girl posing "half undressed" in a suggestive manner. That's why Norma Jeane had moved out. And her husband, she said, had told her she was engaged in something that was unhealthy.

"Unhealthy? I asked, what did he mean by that? She said he meant she was doing something that wasn't wholesome. He didn't approve of her becoming a commercial model. She said he meant that it was cheap. She asked if I thought it was cheap, and I said, 'I'm the guy taking the picture. Where does that put me?' The only thing cheap about what we were doing was the hotdog and tin of aspirins, which didn't mean our professions were cheap by a long shot. She wanted to know if I thought she appeared to be cheap in any way, and I said certainly not. Then, damn it, she seemed like she was in pain again. Her moods swung back and forth, being down one minute then beaming back and only to start getting bothered again. She was like a baby and I figured it had to be that kind of day—a bad day all around...

"I told her most men would be very happy to have a young wife as pretty as she was—and being a model to boot. I said it would surely arouse them and they'd never stray far. I was kidding a little to get her cheered, and then she said her husband didn't share that theory. She hated being married because she personally had no concern about being a housewife whether they got aroused or not. She was getting a divorce because she was so miserable, and so sad at times she wanted to kill herself.

"I must've looked shocked and she said she wasn't going to do it. She didn't want anyone to tell her how she should live or behave which is what her husband was doing, and she didn't want anyone telling her how she should make a living because she was on her own. I told her she was damned right and with the war going on she had to do the best she could."

Norma Jeane later confided to Joe Jasgur, another photographer, that while she was having success as a model, "having a lucky break," as she called it, she confessed she sometimes would "get down in the dumps," like the feeling would come over her that there seemed to be "no answer to anything..." Jasgur said he didn't know what she was talking about. He later made the claim that Norma Jeane had asked him to marry her (while in the throes of divorcing Dougherty), but he'd had to turn her down. He also made the claim that she had six toes.

She spent her twentieth birthday in Las Vegas, Nevada, waiting out

the six weeks' residency requirement for a divorce.

Living again with Aunt Lower, but temporarily, Norma Jean managed to save enough money to move into the Hollywood Studio Club, a boarding house for young women—mostly aspiring actresses like Jacqulyn Cooper from Colorado.

"Nothing was inexpensive," Jacqulyn says, "and you had to do all you could to supplement an income. Norma Jeane was sharing a room, and unlike what she was doing, I didn't elect to model for the more risqué magazines. When I got to Hollywood, I was told being exposed in those magazines could hurt your career if they found out what you were doing. It was almost the same as being a prostitute, and if it got around generally that you posed for those kind of publications—even the general pinup magazines, you wouldn't be taken seriously. Even though there was nothing shameful or obscene about the pictures, you wouldn't find those magazines on someone's coffee table or in the library.

"The photographers were selling Norma Jeane's picture right and left. They found her the most attractive model, the most sought-after, and for her this was an acceptance—a grand approval. She saw nothing wrong with the pinup posing, nothing unsavory about it, but it was still considered less-than-dignified posing. She didn't consider it a hindrance to getting ahead and in fact it made her feel important to be in such demand. But the studio casting directors stayed away from such a model—or for that matter, any figure model because of the censorship issue in movies."

Nikki Morgan from Cincinnati found Hollywood "busy and exciting..." but rather than hustling tables in a boulevard coffee shop, she chose to pursue modeling the same as Norma Jeane, from skimpy two-piece bathing suits and revealing undies to the covers of detective magazines.

"We enjoyed a social life at the Studio Club," says Nikki, "and the friends you made were helpful in getting jobs or getting cues from the usual gossip. The girls were sociable, but their jokes and the games did not draw Marilyn into the group. Her name was still Norma Jeane and her last name Baker, which had been her maiden name. She never seemed comfortable around the other girls who'd be chattering away or even at ease in a group of people. We were all in the same boat except Marilyn. She shied away from get-togethers where the gossip and news was about who was working or the politics of getting ahead, and she didn't respond, except to be polite, and at that always kind of quiet. She stayed off by herself or was out, and didn't share where she'd gone or who she saw. The girls liked to know what one another were up to, but Marilyn didn't show any interest in close friendships. She'd actually blush if you spoke to her, and looked like she wanted to dash from the room. She was always finding a reason to excuse herself, like using the phone. Always running to use the telephone.

"A couple girls I'd seen her listening to, then I talked to as well. She had a fresh, scrubbed quality about her but she was always late and nerv-

ous and out of breath. We went for breakfast around the corner because she didn't cook or eat at the club. She'd have to join the others in the kitchen, and if she did not go out, then she went off by herself in her room. She was strange, a strange girl. She wouldn't eat much—a slice of toast or a poached egg. No butter or jam on the toast, and her coffee without any cream or sugar. I didn't know what the pills were she was taking. I figured they were vitamins. White capsules. She told me she had to take a sleeping pill to kick staying awake half the night. She said sometimes the pills knocked her out and she wouldn't even hear her alarm clock.

"But she appeared determined in what she was after and she was having success with it. Everywhere you looked you saw Norma Jeane on a magazine, more than the other models, and she was working most of the time. No one got rich from those cheapskate photographers who kept calling, wanting more…half the time more than just taking pictures."

In November of '45, Marilyn was hired through the agency to model for Andre De Dienes. "This man was well-known, "Nikki says. "He spent days shooting Marilyn. Once she looked sheepish and said he'd told her he was in love with her.

"We were in the drugstore and even the guy behind the counter said he'd seen her on a magazine. We were on Sunset Boulevard and then walked to the drive-in and sat inside. She said she would make a good carhop, and I said, 'I bet you would,' and she said she was serious. She could make more money than doing what she was doing. If nothing else happened, she said she'd apply for a job. I don't know whether she did or not, though I told her the way she'd walk around wagging her tail she'd make a mint.

"Only once did we talk about guys and she said she was having an affair with a photographer. This is the famous guy who said he was in love with her. She said, 'He says I am the spring in someone's life.' They went to the beach and had stayed overnight somewhere north by the mountains. They'd had dinner and breakfast in a café in Mojave, and she laughed and said, 'He wants to marry me!' I asked if she was going to do it, and she said, 'Of course not!' As though I'd asked if she was going to flap her wings and fly to the moon. She looked at me and said, 'There isn't any way in the world somebody's going to make me go through all that again…'"

Norma Jeane was getting so much work as model, Jacqulyn says, "I jokingly asked her what her secret was, though I didn't really have to ask but I wanted to know more about what she was up to. She said she didn't have a secret. I said she could tell me because I won't breathe a word if you're having more affairs with these fellows. She said 'Absolutely not!' and what did I think she was? Very bothered, like that, like I'd hurt her feelings even wondering if she was sleeping with these fellows. In fact, she was so bothered she didn't pay any attention to me for days.

"I saw her in the restaurant of the Roosevelt Hotel on the boulevard and she was talking to a well-dressed man who looked familiar to me but I couldn't remember his name. She was wearing sunglasses that had a white frame and were pointed on the ends like a cat's eyes. I didn't intrude but when they parted, she came to where I was seated, all excited and exuberant, and said she was going to Twentieth Century Fox movie studio where it was possible a screen test could be arranged for her. 'You're kidding!' I said and I hugged her and congratulated her. 'I'll be praying they put you in a movie,' I said, and she said she was praying for the test but there was nothing definite about a movie. Not yet, she said and gave me a big smile that was like somebody'd switched on a light. I told her, 'Honey, you deserve every darned thing that's good in this world.'"

Ben Lyon, then head of new talent at Fox, was eager to meet the girl gracing the covers of a couple dozen magazines sitting on his desk. He wadded them into a cabinet behind his chair when the secretary said, "Miss Baker has finally arrived." Lyon sat back. "Send her in," he said.

A nervous Norma Jeane bubbled apologies for being an hour late, stuttered and offered excuses but Lyon said, "Relax—relax." He wasn't bothered and to ease her tension he said, "I was late getting in here myself." He told her who he was, what he did and why he did it, and finally said, "Tell me a little about yourself, Norma Jeane—" then creaked back in the chair as she jittered and stuttered into a monologue he found both fascinating and disconcerting.

Interrupting her, he told her what he had in mind: a simple test on film. She wanted to know what she was supposed to do, and he said, "This is just for us to get an idea of how you photograph, how you move and look on motion picture film." There would be no dialogue, no sound.

"She answered questions," Lyon said later, "with a forthright honesty and bluntness I found refreshing. She blushed, was perspiring, and obviously anxious, fidgeting, but frankly I found her openness and truthfulness surprising and refreshing." She had done no acting, she said, had never taken a lesson and knew nothing about the craft or the making of movies. But she had seen movies all her life and loved movies more than anything. Lyon asked who she loved the most in the movies and she said Jean Harlow.

"My guardian," she said, "or who used to be my guardian, Miss Grace McKee—well, she's married now so her name is Grace Goddard and she's in West Virginia—she always told me someday I would be like Jean Harlow..."

Smiling, Lyon said, "You know who I am?"

She nodded. "You were in *Hell's Angels* with Jean Harlow. You were wonderful."

"I wouldn't go that far," he said, "but thanks. So you've thought about becoming a movie star?"

Norma Jeane smiled and said, "That is probably something I have always thought about, Mr. Lyon ..."

Throwing practicality and protocol to the wind because he had not gained the approval from the studio heads to run the test, Lyon arranged for a color shoot of Norma Jeane, convinced it could prove worth the effort.

He didn't like her name. "It was too much like a child's," he said.

"She needed something nice that would offer dignity and offset the little girl feeling about her, but at the same time give some class to the physical appeal."

Though Lyon was well aware of the youth and pureness Marilyn seemed to radiate, he also believed she showed a playful awareness of her own arresting sex appeal, also radiating like a heater cranked to jack volume. She did understand what she had, knowing if she kept the two apart, but like Siamese twins, not too far apart—the innocence and the sexuality—she could be sitting on top of the world.

At Ben Lyon's beach house

Marilyn and Diana Herbert

Getting into the Movies

Darryl Zanuck watched the screen test and said, "So what?" Singular in his lack of appreciation, he said, "She's a magazine pinup girl who's so overexposed it's pathetic. She's never acted. We're a movie studio and what're we going to do with a pinup cutie?"

It wasn't only the sex angle, Ben Lyon tried to explain. There was a kind of glowing quality to the girl, a backyard barn maiden or the kid next door, once you get some clothes on her. Her skin's almost luminous and her smile is like lights going on. Lyon wasn't the only vote in favor of a contract for Marilyn. Impatiently, Zanuck said, "Fine. Sign her on a minimum contract and the horse shit's on your hands."

Diana Herbert was the daughter of writer F. Hugh Herbert, under contract to Fox. Herbert had written *The Moon is Blue*, other movies and Broadway plays, then wrote and directed *Scudda Hoo! Scudda Hay!* for Fox, in which Marilyn was cast with a single line.

June Haver, Marilyn Monroe, Colleen Townsend, and F. Hugh Herbert

"My father's picture was Marilyn's first," says Diana. "She was a scared rabbit. The front office had dismissed her and thought of her—if they ever thought of her—in a way that was subliminal and would undermine her confidence. Once they felt they had a player's confidence diminished, they'd be less demanding and aggressive and maybe satisfied being a stable player. They thought of Marilyn as just the scatterbrain daydreamer they believed her to be. They called her a frump. I wasn't sure what a frump was, but soon realized it was someone who couldn't take a stand and could be counted on to deliver what you wanted while the using was good. Soon as it dried up they'd be through with her as they had been with dozens of people. So they were saying she's a frump and certainly one of the best frumps and maybe she'd prove a goose that'd lay some fourteen-karat egg—frump or no frump.

"It was during the shooting of the movie *Scudda Hoo*," says Diana Herbert, "Marilyn's first picture and she sort of

Marilyn Monroe, Colleen Townsend, and F. Hugh Herbert

sidled up to me, like girl to girl. It was always like we were sharing some secrets we had to keep from the rest of the world. We'd go to the commissary and she wouldn't talk to other people, just kind of all gathered in. If she did say hello it was like she was embarrassed. I really honestly couldn't determine if it was a case of drastic shyness—and there was that, yes—or more of a fear to be overheard, like she was going to share a dastardly secret, and if she let truth be known, we'd explode or something. Basically we became friendly from *Scudda Hoo*, and poor Marilyn's little part got cut from the picture, but she'd done the work and was excited and proud.

"On the sly, I snuck her into a screening room where my father was viewing for editing, and Marilyn got to see herself in the bit part before it was trimmed from the picture. She'd had one line and whispered to me, 'Do I sound that awful?' There wasn't anything awful about it all. I said she had a lovely voice—soft and appealing. My father, using the old adage, told me Marilyn photographed like a million dollars. He told me she was going to be a big star if they didn't crowd or rush her into it. He said she had every ingredient for it built right into her by nature."

Though under a standard stock player contract, Marilyn wasn't attending the Fox drama school. Diana Herbert, though not under contract, was attending because of her father. "A kid of school away from school," says Diana. "I wanted to be an actress more than anything in the world, and I had this marvelous door open for me, through my dad.

"I guess we first came together when I was preparing, for weeks, it seemed, a song I'd sing at a talent show for the rest of the studio. I wanted to sing 'Johnny One Note' from Rodgers and Hart's Babes in Arms, but they had me singing, 'I Never Took a Lesson in My Life'..."

Two days before the show was to go on, Diana was told she wasn't going to be doing the song. A contract player named Marilyn Monroe was going to perform for the talent show. "They were giving Marilyn the push," says Diana, "but I was heart-sunk, and then surprised because so was Marilyn, heart sunk that she was doing the song I'd worked so hard on, and heart sunk that she'd have to be performing for 'all those people,' as she put it, singing a song she didn't even know. She asked if I'd help her learn the lyrics in time. Maybe someone else would've been mad about her being put in their place but she was so genuinely sad about it I felt sorry for her—not even for myself."

In January the daily newspapers carried promotional plugs about Marilyn Monroe—"Eighteen year old native daughter of Hollywood has been working as a commercial model and baby sitter until she went to the home of a movie talent scout to sit a baby. Now she is under contract with a studio and going to the studio drama school for one year before being assigned to play a role in front of the camera."

Marilyn said, "I've never sat with a baby in my life, not that I wouldn't want to, I love babies..."

While Marilyn was getting a buildup, supervised by Lyon, Diana was preparing to leave for New York to appear in a Broadway play. She and her sister had planned a swimming party at their Copra del Orr Road home in Bel Air, inviting Marilyn who whispered her acceptance. "Oh, yes," she said. "I would be delighted to be there."

Diana says, "The other guests were mostly young like all of us, and they knew who Marilyn was—the publicity and magazines, plus the couple other pictures she was working in. Everyone at the party showed their excitement about Marilyn showing up—especially in a bathing suit and swimming with them." So much time passed from when Marilyn was expected, that Diana's guests had forgotten she was coming. "I'd told them she was a friend," Diana says, "and they were looking at me with raised eyebrows...

"Some of them were still swimming," she says, "but most had left the pool for the buffet supper. Somehow Marilyn appeared, having come in through the back way to the property, and she was off behind the dressing room across from the pool. She said she was sorry about being late and I said that was fine, but she said she'd forgotten her bathing suit. I said that was okay, too, because I had a brand new suit she could use. She said 'oh, fine,' and she'd change into it in the dressing room.

"So far, no one else had seen her, most having wandered from the pool and up to the house. Two or three were still splashing around, and I had to go to the house and see to the party. I thought it was strange that Marilyn was taking so long changing into a bathing suit. What was she going to do—be swimming by herself? It was so late already. People were enjoying the buffet, and they'd kept saying, Oh, sure, sure, where's Marilyn Monroe? Laughing about it, like I'd made it up.

"Two or three times I want down to the dressing room and knocked on the door. I asked if she was all right. Was she coming out? She'd speak close to the other side of the door, saying she'd be right out. 'Oh, yes, I'm coming right out,' she'd say.

"She didn't come out," Diana says. "I have to confess I was worried and for almost an hour and a half or close to two hours, Marilyn was alone in the dressing room. God knows what was taking her so long. And then—then—she disappeared. She wasn't there anymore. She'd snuck out and taken off around the back of the house to wherever she'd parked her car—if in fact she'd parked a car. I don't know. What I know is that she came to the party and nobody saw her, and then she stayed for almost two hours alone in the pool dressing room. I have no idea what she'd been doing in there. Sitting? Standing? Waiting for what? Afraid to come out? Alone and responding to me in that hushed tone that she'd be right out, and she never came out, except to disappear.

She was almost ignored on the Fox lot. She possibly did a few extra bits, moving across a dance floor, at a table in a night club. She said, "I did just what Jean Harlow did..." Tony Curtis would do the same at Universal, "like dancing around the room in a scene," and whatever line he'd had was cut from the print.

Through Lyon's urging, Marilyn appeared in a small, credited role as a hash-house waitress in *Dangerous Years*, with Darryl Hickman and Scotty Beckett, the actor who went from being a kid star to an "inconclusive" suicide.

Hickman thought she was "very attractive but standoffish without acting like she meant to be that way... It was like you'd say, hey, she's got some other scene going and it's nothing to do with a movie. Not to say she wasn't sweet, but kind of goofy, you know? She seemed to spook easily and get upset over something going wrong that didn't mean anything."

Diana says, "Marilyn couldn't defend herself well, and she didn't know how to play the game at the studio. She figured they'd come to her but what happens when you adopt that attitude is they forget about you until the bookkeeper says it's time to clean out the stables. They cleaned them out and almost as soon as she thought she'd be getting another part, the sons of bitches didn't pick up her option. She was out of a job."

Michael Owen, actor and brief suitor of the unemployed Marilyn, says, "I felt sorry for her. She wanted to work in the pictures more than she wanted to breathe, practically. Landing any studio contract was a dream come true. It was the pot of gold at the end of rainbow. We met at Schwab's drugstore on Sunset and went out a few times, drove around in the old car I had. We talked but I honestly don't think she ever listened to what I was saying, and I'm not sure what the heck she talked about. She didn't want to make a display of us seeing each other, because she said though she enjoyed the company there were others that might 'not understand.'

"Understand what? She'd say something like 'There are particular things a person has to do,' and that she had to do them. She said, 'It doesn't make any difference,' but I didn't know what she was saying. I felt pretty quick that if I pressed at it she'd skitter off with some nonsense or she'd tell me there was somebody else she was involved with. That part I got the heebie-jeebies about because I believe I cared for her more than I probably should have if I'd had any sense, but I didn't have any sense.

"I had another job as well and I made pretty good, so we'd eat and she'd gobble down a hamburger or a grilled cheese, and I even managed to give her some rent money. I bought her a dress and shoes on Hollywood Boulevard for her birthday, though her birthday had come and gone before I met her, so she said, 'It can be for my next birthday!' That made sense. She wanted to dress classy and go to clubs on the Strip, like we went to La Rue's, and I remember she talked to a couple important people—agents, guy that were out of my class. She didn't introduce me.

"She was young and outstandingly pretty and she was an operator. I thought of that expression about getting something in a bottle and making a mint. Our conversations were always about her—she was her favorite subject once you got past the small-talk stage. She went on about what she wanted, what she thought she wasn't getting and how she had things planned to get more of what she wanted. She meant working in pictures. That was the most important thing in the world to her.

"I couldn't argue with her self-serving ideas. I was an actor but I wasn't Ronald Coleman or Spencer Tracy, and I believe in her own mind she was seeing herself on that level—up there on that rung of the ladder.

"The thing is, this girl, for the short time I saw her, was very resistant to any physical demonstration of feelings. She said she didn't want that kind of relationship. Okay, I know it's been said ad infinitum that Marilyn was sleeping around and that she slept her way to where she got, even for bedding and grub, but I am reluctant to accept that hype because that wasn't part of her chemistry. No matter what's said, that bill of goods won't be sold to me. In the brief time we spent together, and yes, I knew I wasn't the only one in her rosy picture of the movie world, I got to know her a little and I like to think I saw this fairy princess more clearly than some of these who say so much about her. She was blessed by God with a beauty that was stunning, and she threw herself into things but kind of without focusing on the outcome or the conclusion of something...

"We kissed a few times and I wanted her for real but she was preoccupied when it came to actually wanting something from her like an expression of a mutual caring. I don't think it was possible for her to really care about the person she was seeing—whoever it was, except in her own thinking, and how she saw it which wasn't necessarily the way things were. Like she'd think she cared for somebody but it wasn't anything she'd be able to get across to that person.

"Marilyn was a needy creature, and wanted to be helped in a way like being taken care of while she chased her dreams. I mean, we talked but I don't think she was capable of having any idea about practicalities, like bills and leases or keeping appointments or stuff like that. I'd wait for her two hours. She'd show and say she couldn't wake up because she'd had to take a sleeping pill the night before, or she'd had to wash her hair soon as she got out of bed...

"I said I believed maybe there was more to life than the movies and she just looked at me, not saying she disagreed, but wouldn't or couldn't give me an argument. I knew she wasn't able to entertain what I was saying...

"She was almost helpless at giving of herself to a situation. I don't think Marilyn was capable of conducting a meaningful relationship, other than one that served her and by that I don't mean to imply she was conniving, but only that she felt comfortable in a situation where she could feel convinced that her best interests were being taken care of...

"I saw how easy it was for someone with an ulterior motive to hook up with Marilyn, convincing her it was in her best interest and winning her confidence that you really cared. She'd be manipulated for personal gain as would happen again and again, and Marilyn, who was unable to give to a relationship, would be left holding an empty bag when the game was played out—as all games are in Hollywood. They all play out.

"She was somehow all alone, like the streetwalker you've used to the hilt and underpaid in the bargain. She moved from one place to another like in and out of a revolving door, and then she was gone out of my life as quick as she'd come in... I knew I never made even a ripple in her life. She was something beyond all of us and I am grateful that I spent the time I did with her. I'm sorry I couldn't have given her something substantial to hold on to, which she always seemed to want but she wouldn't take it because she never trusted you...

"My life is richer for having known her. I can still see her sitting across from me, the candle burning in that French café on Sunset, drinking champagne. We drove the beach one time and she had champagne in a milk bottle.

"She changed something in me and I only wish I could have changed something in her. But it wasn't me to do it, and it wasn't really anyone to do it. She belonged to that Grecian concept of being with the gods."

"Ladies of the Chorus"

A Neon Valentine

James Dean would call it the "revolving meat rack—" that Hollywood party circuit passing young people around like loaves popping out of an oven, or like pretty and dumb horses turning on a merry-go-round.

Marilyn, however, twenty-one, prettier than most and far from dumb, proved disarming to seventy year old Joe Schenck. He was ex-husband of silent star Norma Talmadge, founder of 20th Century Productions and one of the most influential men in motion pictures.

With fresh, bright-faced eagerness, Marilyn accompanied another girl to one of Schenck's well-known poker parties. "You'll serve as kind of hostesses," she was told, "and meet all kinds of important people."

Schenck said to Marilyn, "Come and sit beside me, young lady, and tell me about yourself." She sat beside Schenck and told him everything she could. Elderly Schenck couldn't help feeling she was like his granddaughter, and later said to Pat DiCicci, an associate and handyman at supplying girls for parties, "This one has an electric quality... She sparkles and bubbles like a fountain. She's very different from the other ones and I feel drawn to her. What was her name again?"

"Marilyn," he was told.

She wanted to be a movie actress. She told Schenck she wasn't a "nobody" because she'd been under contract to Fox and had been in two movies. "Well—one," she said, "that you can actually see me in."

Schenck told her he believed she had all the right qualifications to be in movies and have a successful career. She thanked him, and then he said, "Why are you at the party?"

"Out of work," she said, and "without a roof."

"I got a lot of roofs," Schenck said. "You want one? I'll get a roof put over your head."

"Oh," Marilyn said, "I'd be most thankful, Mr. Schenck, if you could let me have one of your roofs. It doesn't have to be a very big roof..."

Inviting her to stay temporarily in a guest cottage behind his

Holmby Hills estate, Schenck said, "You need someone looking after your interests, Marilyn. You're a very attractive and a remarkable girl but you can't just run around without someone taking care of you..." Later he told her, "You don't have to worry about things because I'll fix it for you. Just give me a little time to get it straight and I'll see that you are working again."

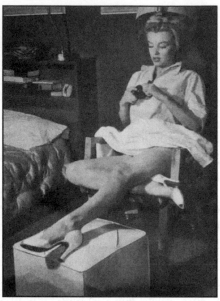

Unlike the usual fishing-line sinkers, "Uncle Joe's" proclamations came fourteen karat. He convinced poker pal Harry Cohn, head of Columbia Pictures, to sign Marilyn to a six-month contract and "give the girl a break..."

Almost overnight, Marilyn found herself signing a short-term contract at Columbia. She said to Schenck, "How am I ever going to be able to thank you enough for caring about me...?"

"You be everything you can," he said, "and that's how you can thank me."

To hate Harry Cohn, Columbia's "big cheese," as he was called, it was said that you had to stand in a long line. Marilyn later recalled about the mogul that shortly after she was cast in a picture, was getting a pay check and an apartment, she turned down Cohn's invitation to spend a weekend on his boat. He had called Marilyn into his office, showed her a photograph of his boat and told her he was thinking of another picture she'd be right for—about a bathing beauty who becomes Miss America. He asked Marilyn to remove her clothes down to her panties so he could have look at her "shape."

Marilyn said, "I told Mr. Cohn I couldn't do that because I never wore panties, and after that incident, Mr. Cohn didn't want to talk to me any more. He was like on the other side of the moon or somewhere... After that I started wearing panties but then I thought I don't want to do this, so I didn't wear them anymore."

Marilyn's single movie at Columbia was *Ladies of the Chorus*, an important role for her. While otherwise unremarkable and unsuccessful, the film contains a pivotal scene between Marilyn and Adele Jergens, playing Marilyn's mother, that is performed impeccably by Marilyn. It is a performance that in no way could have been improved upon. She is believable and unforgettable. In another scene Marilyn sings beautifully and offers a haunting, solitary dance number that seems as if she is drifting out of a dream.

Rand Brooks, featured in *Chorus*, recalled the day Marilyn brought her mother to the studio. "I met this frail lady named Mrs. Baker," he said, "who hardly spoke but her eyes got big... She was nervous to be on a set, watching her daughter work in the movie. Marilyn was so proud of herself and eager for her mother to see how she had become a success. Mrs. Baker didn't say very much. She was polite but withdrawn, like in awe over the whole experience. I don't imagine the average person appreciates how much time goes into making even a fifteen second scene in a picture... With Marilyn, sometimes it got a little difficult because she wasn't sure she was doing something right and to her best advantage. She was very nervous and suffered a terrible stage fright, but she was great. I don't believe at the time she was aware of how good she was. She had done bits at Fox but she was always green and unsure of herself. Twentieth hadn't appreciated her and, in fact, it wasn't much different at Columbia..."

Natasha Lytess working with Marilyn

While she was filming *Chorus*, Columbia's drama coach, Natasha Lytess, kept working with Marilyn and coaching from the sidelines. Natasha claimed the Russian school of acting, swore by the old-style actors, but had been vitally impressed with Marilyn since the moment they'd met. She so believed in Marilyn's potential that in a short time she

Clockwise: Bernice Miracle, Mona Miracle, Grace Goddard, Grace's sister Enic Knebelkamp, Marilyn, "Aunt" Ana, and Gladys; Pacific Seas Cafeteria on South Olive, celebrating Marilyn's divorce from Jim Dougherty. September 13, 1946

would uncompromisingly dedicate herself to helping Marilyn develop her potential. Later, she said later, "I believed in Marilyn completely. I knew from the start the talents she possessed, though they were bound-up by the girl's wretched upbringing…

"When Columbia dropped her, it hurt her badly and I made the decision that I would devote the time I had left to guiding Marilyn in her efforts…It was that important. Something to be done and someone had to do it, like the discovery of a new star in the heavens. The darkness has to be lifted so the light could shine through."

Though Harry Cohn talked himself into announcing that a further investment in Marilyn wasn't worth it, *Ladies of the Chorus* proved an important step for Marilyn. The short term contract dead-ended, and Rand Brooks said, "They were nuts but don't tell him I said so. Columbia lost a valuable property, but I wouldn't try to understand something that was way out of my control…"

Looking back at her Columbia stint, Marilyn said, "I sincerely thought I would be working more than I did. I was quite disappointed with how it turned out when I was expected to perform in a manner that had nothing to do with appearing in front of the camera…and that was supposed to be an act of self-promotion."

Johnny Hyde escorting Marilyn to "stardom"

Falling for Marilyn

Johnny Hyde, a small, frail, Russian son of a circus acrobat came to America in the early 1900s and grew to a pint-sized man, but took after Marilyn like a full-scale steamroller.

An important theatrical agent, Hyde almost single-handedly raised movie stars as one might grow hot-house orchids. Stars like Rita Hayworth and Betty Hutton, Lana Turner and Esther Williams, owed their success to Johnny Hyde of the William Morris Agency. He represented Bob Hope, and brought blonde Mary Beth Hughes to the top of her career. In fact it was the same thing about Mary Beth Hughes that Hyde first felt in seeing Marilyn. He said, "She's a cross between Mary Beth and Lana Turner..." Vice president of William Morris when he met Marilyn, Hyde laid out a personal red carpet. By hook or crook he determined he'd make her a star as big as Lana Turner or Jean Harlow. He'd shove her down the producers' throats.

"A sixth sense is what he had," says George Litto, an agent with William Morris when he represented the author as an actor in New York during the 1950s. Litto later moved to the coast to open his own agency in Beverly Hills, then produced films such as *Dressed to Kill, Blow Out* and *Kansas* for Warner Bros., and more under contract with Fox.

"Not too many in the business had the moxie Johnny had," says Litto. "The relationship between Marilyn and Hyde wasn't a secret to anybody except in the beginning to Hyde's wife and family. It was no secret either that Marilyn was on the scene with whoever could get her ahead. I'd met her but didn't have the time to get involved in her needs. You had to have it in your nature to be that attentive to someone so dependent and wanting constant attention."

Johnny Hyde was that kind of guy, housing a wide, accommodating and sympathetic streak for certain individuals, recalled another agent with William Morris. "Hyde met Marilyn at a party given by Sam Spiegel. She'd accompanied actor John Carroll and his wife, Lucille Ryman, an MGM talent scout, who knew Johnny Hyde."

Marilyn had been living with the Carrolls for several months, accepting their kindness and a weekly stipend. Carroll later said, "We cared about her. She was lost, hungry and out of work. She needed someone to look out for her and take some care of her. Lucille and I did the same for a number of young hopefuls trying to break into pictures, though Marilyn stayed with us the longest... When Lucille introduced Marilyn to Johnny, his eyes lit up and he immediately gobbled Marilyn into his life. That was it."

In a short time, Hyde was telling Marilyn she was the "most exciting female" he had ever met. He laid it right out that there was nothing he wouldn't do for her. He took her to Palm Springs, bought her clothes, furs, jewelry. He paid the rent for her hotel on Olympic Boulevard and told her he would make her a star. "I have it in my power to do that," he said. "I don't mean a contract player, I mean a *star*." He said she'd be up there with Joan Crawford.

Hyde's efforts were as astonishing as was his devotion to Marilyn, thirty years younger than Hyde. He paid all her travel expenses. "Name it," says Litto, "Hyde did it." He made a gaudy, defiant show of Marilyn everywhere he could. She was seen by everybody on the arm of Johnny Hyde—one of the most important men in Hollywood.

Carroll said, "Marilyn told Johnny all she wanted to do was work. She wanted to be in the movies."

Hyde said, "I'll get you a contract at MGM. If that doesn't work, we'll get you back at Fox."

It was plain from the bit Marilyn had with Groucho Marx in *Love Happy*, her hip-rolling stroll across a room that set gyroscopes catawampus, that Johnny Hyde's latest discovery—a girl with a gorgeous innocence—was broadcasting sex waves as loud as beating a bass drum.

Young, beautiful Kathleen Hughes, under contract to Universal, was about to start *Ticket to Tomahawk* with Rory Calhoun. "Something happened," Kathleen says. "I didn't have the part anymore. I said, what's going on? They said the part had been cast—somebody else was doing it. I said who, for god's sake? I was told a girl named Marilyn Monroe. I asked how'd that happen? They said, from powers beyond us. Bullshit, I said. I'm under contact to this studio and they're casting it from outside—with somebody nobody knows?"

I first met Kathleen on the Universal set of *Cult of the Cobra*. Our chat got around to Rory Calhoun who I had known for a few years. Talking about *Ticket to Tomahawk*, Kathleen said, "It was Johnny Hyde who got Marilyn in the picture and since I was still under contract to Fox at the time. Well, it didn't matter as they'd stick me in something else. It didn't have anything to do with me, but the fact is that it was the same with my cousin, Diana. Even though Diana hadn't a contract she was a 'regular' because of her dad—F. Hugh Herbert, who was my uncle. They'd given Marilyn the song at the talent show and just set Diana out in the rain. Well, with *Ticket*, I didn't know all about Marilyn and I hadn't seen *Ladies of the Chorus*, but it was in operation, this thing of replacing someone with Marilyn because of the push she was getting to be moved into the spotlight. That's how it worked. Made me feel better that it was political and not personal."

Kathleen Hughes

Rory Calhoun talked at length about Marilyn while we were at the Ojai ranch he'd bought from wrangler Doc Burkhardt. He said, "*Tomahawk* was the first picture I did with Marilyn and even that one had a lot of problems. I liked her and she was all excited being in the movie... like a little kid the way she bubbled sometimes, but scared as hell—scared of the crew and scared because when she was left on her own she didn't know if she was doing something right or not...

"Problems came up with her in

the studio, and on location which was in Durango where she got sick. I swore she had stomach poisoning because of so much pain she seemed to be having. Like someone being tortured. She said she had to take a lot of penicillin but the doctor told her it wasn't wise. He was saying a person's system couldn't handle that much, but Marilyn said it was okay. She said she could take it and it'd be okay. Like a damn fool she went ahead and took all this penicillin and sure as shit she busted out in penicillin poisoning. I thought, that's goddamn *dumb*! She had rashes all

Rory Calhoun

over and even in her crotch which she'd talk about in case you were interested in her rashes, and she'd show you if you wanted. I didn't see too many around who weren't interested in looking at her rashes, including me..."

Marilyn was peculiar, Rory said. "This flashy look at you but at the same time she was backing away. It was like she was very timid and if you got bothered with her she'd just about fall apart. She did her best, and that took a while to get her to do it...

"She didn't present herself that she was *trying* to get you interested in a situation with her, and that was just who she was. When you're on the receiving end of behavior like that, you pretty soon have to figure all that much interest has got to do with how *you're* seeing it. Then there was the thing about her getting special treatment. Being very patient with her and running some takes longer than they should've. So why not—what the hell? What did I care?"

If care had ever been an issue, it would rest with Johnny Hyde. In a short time, so enraptured with Marilyn, the agent left his wife and family, rented a separate house in Beverly Hills and moved Marilyn in with him. She kept the Beverly Carlton hotel room to discourage flagrant gossip, but Johnny said he didn't care about the gossip. His concern had to do with a bad heart condition that kept him teetering on the edge of life like an unsure wire walker. The only thing of importance at that stage of his life was Marilyn and he was calling her his own.

After *Ticket to Tomahawk*, and consulting with Lucille Ryman at MGM, Johnny got Marilyn an important small part in a John Huston film, *The Asphalt Jungle*. Near panic, Marilyn went to work with Natasha Lytess for her audition with Huston. "Except for Johnny Hyde and his influence," said Natasha, "no one believed in Marilyn. If it wasn't for Johnny Hyde's involvement, they would treat Marilyn poorly, like an expendable commodity. I knew she would become a success. As a person, she was almost totally without fortitude. You could say she was someone afraid of their own shadow, so terribly insecure, so socially uncomfortable and shy, and never knowing what to say. She would ask me, what she should say?

"I tried to get her to draw upon herself, to go into her own experiences, but I don't believe she did. It was there in the experiences, some place she did not venture to go. Yes, that was it... What I know, I learned from Max Reinhardt, and looking back now, I believe Marilyn denied who she really was, except for her sex appeal which she had confidence in. She knew it worked—she was as graceful with her appeal as a swimmer or ballerina. She knew what she was doing..."

John Huston said, "The girl came in to read for the part in *Asphalt Jungle*, and she was so quiet and timid, but cute and sweet, and something very most precious about her. She was perfect. She hardly had to open her mouth and I knew she was right for the part. She was exceptional. Not a girl who would be run of the mill by far, so she had the part before she knew it, as far as I was concerned. She read once, lying on the floor because in the scene she was supposed to be on a couch and there wasn't a couch in the room where we were. She didn't like the way she read the first time and asked if she could do it again. I said, sure, of course you can, and she did. I said, you can read it as much as you like, my dear. It melted you, she was so right for what I had in mind. I didn't bother reading anyone else for the part. It was one of those moments when the ingredients are perfect and you don't bother looking further. She said to me, 'this will be the most important movie role I will have done.' I said, 'Well, congratulations, Marilyn.' She said she hoped she would do well because she was so pleased I had chosen her. I said, 'you'll do just fine, my dear, you just be yourself and don't worry your head about anything else. You'll do fine.'"

Later, Huston said, "There's a truth she has that's absolutely profound. It's all the girl has." Huston said there was some combination in her performance that tapped an individual, vulnerable quality that no one else could get at. "It was right there," he said, "radiating off the screen like some bright searchlight, and there wasn't one single, deliberate thing about it..."

With Mickey Rooney

Hyde tried for an MGM contract for Marilyn, but the studio was reluctant at first, and Hyde took her back to Fox. When MGM did make an offer, according to George Litto, Hyde bumped the figure from stock player and Metro wanted time to consider and offer a counter deal.

In the meantime, Hyde pushed and pulled, bantered and bartered every favor from those in his debt to keep Marilyn working. He believed if he kept her working, the world would soon take notice. "Only a matter of time," he told Marilyn.

Litto says, "Metro later regretted the decision not to grab her soon after *Asphalt Jungle*, but the picture was considered a gloomy, noir drama and Marilyn more or less went unnoticed initially. It's a *great* picture, but it took a lot of moxie on Hyde's part to put her over the top."

Marilyn was cast in *The Fireball*, a roller derby picture starring Mickey Rooney and Pat O'Brien being filmed at Fox and featuring James Brown.

I got to know James Brown from a picture the following year at Republic, *Missing Women*. Brown said Marilyn was the hottest-looking girl he'd ever seen. "I tried to date her," he told me. "Most of the girls would date and you'd go places, be seen, unless they were so stuck up as many were. That wasn't what Marilyn was like. But when I talked to her about going out she stood there looking at me like I was speaking

Chinese. Was I making some outlandish request? When she understood I was asking for a date, she quickly told me she was very busy. She also said there was someone special she was seeing, and I said something like well, aren't I special? So she said the same thing over, and that she wouldn't want anything to interfere with what she had to do. I said okay and I didn't pursue it, figuring there was time.

"She seemed nervous and when we were talking about Mickey Rooney, she said, 'He's really terrible, isn't he?' She thought he would have been a nice person from all the movies she'd seen him in, like when he was a kid. She got close to me and her breasts were almost poking my chest. Her eyes got like a surprised look, and she said Mickey was saying dirty things to her. She said he'd whispered dirty things and she was frightened of him...

"She didn't have anything going with Mickey Rooney, and that's a fact, though Mickey said some ludicrous things about her later. I didn't know what she was doing with that little encounter between the two of us, like playing some game—playing-acting something I really didn't get the point of. She'd sit there batting her eyes and give you the feeling she was a pretty dumb girl, but then there was this intense, almost secret-like sincerity behind what she'd say, and that left me with the idea this girl is a mystery. She was truly a mystery..."

Hyde managed to wangle Marilyn into a couple more small parts,

both at MGM. A Metro producer said, "People were talking about the little blonde when you walked away from seeing *Asphalt Jungle*. It was Marilyn that stuck in their minds, and when a player's got that going, you're talking a box-office personality. That's what always came right across in those tests made with Marilyn. All she had to do was stand still and look at the camera and she'd won you. It's a breed apart from us mortals."

Marilyn faithfully believed

every word Johnny Hyde said. She believed his love for her was true though she could not return that same love. He wanted to marry her. He pleaded with her, though getting a divorce from his wife would prove a "monumental hurdle…"

Litto says, "She became the most important person in Johnny's life and in some ways he tried to explain that but couldn't. He was willing to burn all bridges behind him and devote his life to Marilyn. 'Poor Hyde,' some were saying. 'He's got it as bad as it gets…'"

"Fuck everyone," Hyde told another agent. "Everything I've ever done can be measured by the single act of what I'm doing right now." He said perhaps he was a fool but he didn't care. Marilyn meant more to him than an "entire civilization of skeptics and their disapproval." He said, "I hate finger waggers and gossipmongers unless they serve a purpose."

He kept saying he would divorce and marry Marilyn. She said she didn't love him like he loved her. He knew that, he said, but it didn't matter. He could drop dead any time and if they were married she'd become a wealthy widow. She'd never have to worry.

Marilyn said she couldn't marry him *because* of that reason. She'd never marry anyone for money. He told her it tore his soul to envision her worrying or to think of her in want, and though he knew she didn't feel as he felt toward her, it was matter of her security he was talking about.

"It made me sad," Marilyn said later. "I cried when he'd tell me how ill he was and I didn't know how to help him except to be what he wanted me to be…except I could never be his wife. I cared so very much for him but I couldn't marry him for his money or let him hurt his family or himself because of the way he felt about me."

Litto says, "It was no secret that the girl could make a lot of money for someone but that wasn't Johnny's priority. That was a byproduct of his obsession over Marilyn."

She had no interest in being Mrs. Johnny Hyde—the girl who destroyed Johnny's marriage and family, and despite speculation based on groundless rumors, Marilyn was not "sleeping her way through Hollywood..."

"I'm not a *nobody*," she told people. "I was under contract to Twentieth Century Fox and I've made movies—" Any sexual entanglement was just that—an *entanglement* she'd enter into like a cat crossing a litter of broken bottles. Always a dangerous place for Marilyn.

Personal contact with her was riddled with surprises. She could show you she cared and if she didn't care she could play it convincingly enough for the time it took her to get what she wanted. Sylvia Barnhart, who Marilyn was visiting once a week to have the dark roots of her hair bleached, says, "I called her the 'iron butterfly' because she

knew what she was after and she'd hold out for that. She'd settle for nothing less. She was stubborn about people doing what she wanted them to do for her. She used people and they used her..."

Marilyn's life represented a series of chaotic experiences, each one not unfolding into the next but moving *beyond* the last. If an old one held some lingering value, she might go back to it but only briefly. She would take from each situation whatever made her feel secure enough to step forward into another situation. There was nothing personal about her encounters, other than her need to feel accepted as she

111

envisioned herself.

Disappointing for many, Marilyn's need for care did not maneuver her into sexual relationships for their own sake, or for love. Those needs had been scoured away by what she considered her "unexceptional past." Marilyn was as *Marilyn* could be, no one holding her for any length of time— no more than a beautiful, friendly bird can be grounded with lasting success unless it is damaged or its wings are clipped. Marilyn ran from potentially dominating or damaging relationships. She knew the earmarks well, and instinctively she'd step aside.

She cared only on her own terms, not always knowing what her terms were. She play-acted terms. Her commitment, as well as she could grant it, would be for as long as she could bestow attention, which was never very long.

Those very few who managed to be close to Marilyn sensed this. They made no emotional requests and were allowed to hold their place as people she'd need when she needed them. These are the people who did not lift the lid on Marilyn. If anyone wanted to know her better, to know everything about her and make an everlasting bond, Marilyn, the bird, would fly. At the first sign of someone trying to peek beneath that lid Marilyn would bolt, locking down so you could not see into her. The demons then lay undisturbed for a spell.

"I was attending a musical at the Philharmonic downtown," says

Barnhart, "and ran into Marilyn and Johnny Hyde. I spoke to her and she said, 'Do I know you?' That upset me and I said, 'Well, you *should* know me, we've been working together for years and I'm the one who made you the color you are!' And Johnny said, 'Of course she knows you, Sylvia, and you've done a wonderful job with her.' Marilyn said she was sorry but there were so many people—they were all around her. She said, 'I'm so sorry, Sylvia...' The next week when she came in— two hours late as usual, and said her usual thing of, 'Oh, I'm so sorry I'm late but I was in casting...'"

Marilyn strained through her life to hold the facade intact, but carried doubts that she could achieve the impossible goal of being on the outside herself—*Marilyn* the glamour queen, desiring artistic accomplishment as well as popular success. Sylvia would tell her, "You're going to get what you want. Stick to your guns and you'll get what you want."

The pain of the effort could be numbed again and again but she had to hold onto the façade, to have it cemented as an unshakable ambiance, unless, dreadfully, she went as crazy as her mother—or her grandmother—or her grandfather. Or perhaps which she feared most, her father, whoever he might've been. He held a hollow, bleeding place in her soul as a cry that would never be answered. She said, "You know, if you're drowning in the ocean and you cry for help you want somebody to throw you a life buoy, but if there is no one there then you are all alone, aren't you? You will perish, won't you?"

The *Marilyn* mannequin she created stifled the cries within the beautiful shell, sealed tightly and painted pretty, a picture of the most sought-after girl in the world.

Johnny Hyde, her pocket-sized knight in shining armor, wanted Marilyn as his private property more than he'd wanted anything else. On another level, though, the idea of marriage to Marilyn was like climbing aboard a sinking ship. He told her she had to stop taking sleeping pills every night. She had to stop taking pills to wake herself up. No more pills, period. He said, "You drink too much."

She said "I'm always thirsty."

He said, "Thirsty from the pills." The drinking and the pills were a rotten combination. Johnny Hyde had seen it a hundred times.

Marilyn returned his care and concern with an undivided allegiance. He was her mentor, the one whose guidance she could trust. He was more important to her than anyone else. He loved the Marilyn she created and his love solidified her creation. She didn't have to prove who she really was. It was bliss to be totally appreciated as the character she wanted to be and to get what she wanted.

Hedy Lamarr and Joseph Schenck

Hyde never really touched the Marilyn beneath the lid. He sensed her troubles, the chronic insecurities. He tried to convince her that the coming fame he *knew* to be hers would eradicate her doubts and fears. It would erase the nightmares and fill the emptiness she carried. He would see to that. She was, he said, a truly worthwhile human being.

Through Joe Schenck's influence at Fox, Johnny landed Marilyn a part in *All About Eve*. He tried for a second contract for Marilyn but Darryl Zanuck claimed he was still unimpressed. Johnny said, "He'll bend. You get hot enough and even metal bends."

Marilyn and Johnny were looking forward to Palm Springs for a sunny Christmas. His family thought he would be in New York. Instead, shortly before the holidays, Johnny suffered a massive heart attack. He was hospitalized and his family would not allow Marilyn to see him.

"He was calling, 'Marilyn! Marilyn!' before he died," Natasha said. "When word that Johnny had not survived reached Marilyn, she told me, 'He's died so fast it's like the world has crashed apart... If I had not met him he would be alive and with his family...and now I'm alone.' I told her you're not alone. I'm with you, Marilyn. I had to keep telling her 'you're not alone' because I believed she was about to end her life."

She was *always* alone, said *All About Eve* director Joseph Mankiewicz. "She was the most alone person I've known, and *lonely*. The girl suffered with loneliness, but she wouldn't join in get-togethers and always seemed to run off by herself...She didn't make friends and she wasn't sociable. When we were on location, she'd hide in hotel rooms..."

Marilyn was banned from Hyde's funeral by his widow. The clothes, jewelry, the house, the money—anything Hyde had bestowed upon Marilyn was confiscated by Hyde's widow. Marilyn was shut out of their lives. Alone in another hotel room, she suffered the loss of her faithful warrior by drinking and taking pills and wondering if life was worth living. All the pains of her past were reawakened. She took more pills, chewing them apart. "She felt worthless," said Natasha. "She thought she was responsible for Hyde's heart attack. If he had not loved her and cared so much he would be alive..."

Zanuck said, "She knew Hyde had a weak ticker and the self-centered bitch fucked him to death."

She left the hotel and returned to stay with Natasha, the coach more than willing to open her arms to Marilyn. For a brief time, she again welcomed the comfort of elderly Joe Schenck, who spoke only highly of Hyde. Others were saying Johnny had been a great agent but a fool as a man to have fallen for the "blonde dumbbell," as Zanuck referred to her.

Schenck was comfortable with Marilyn. He held her and stroked her head. He caressed her face. She was sad and troubled that what Johnny had started with her career had come to a shattering standstill. Schenck picked up the phone. He knew what would make the girl happy.

It was a trade-off between Schenck and Marilyn. Sex wasn't bound to it. She was there, she filled that place in him, and he luxuriated in the tender moments. Schenck could close his eyes and drift in the heady atmosphere. He didn't need an erect penis. He had Marilyn's care and respect and what could be fudged over the line and called *love*. Smart Schenck, the wise old bird, knew the bliss wouldn't last. Soon he'd be dead like Hyde. Schenck could drink in the girl's care in the doses he was getting without expecting another tomorrow.

Marilyn was exceptional because she *did* care. She thought of this man as a human being, a man who was wise and had experienced pain and hurt. A man like Joe Schenck was the shadowed reflection of a father, as was the elder Louis Calhern who played with the gorgeous young blonde in *Asphalt Jungle*, a role bestowed upon her by Johnny Hyde—who had abandoned her by dying.

A Streetcar Named Disappointment

Marilyn met Elia Kazan in '51 while she was making *As Young as You Feel*. The director, Harmon Jones, previously one of the top editors at Fox, had edited *Gentlemen's Agreement*, *Panic in the Streets*, and *Pinky* for Kazan before stepping into directing.

Albert Dekker, a fine actor I'd met in '55, worked in *As Young as You Feel* and years later told me Kazan wasn't interested in Marilyn as far as putting her in a movie. "He was lending support to Harmon, who wasn't going to shake the world as a director, and Kazan said Marilyn was a beautiful girl but she was going to have trouble with it. I asked him what he meant by saying 'it,' and what kind of trouble apart from being a pain in the ass half the time as she had about the worst chronic stage fright I'd ever seen. Some people get all tensed up when the camera rolls and by the time they hear 'action' they're ready to leap hurdles. Well, Marilyn was sort of the opposite insofar as she would sort of *shrink* into a zombie-like state, but then, well, either she wouldn't remember what she was supposed to say or she'd come to life like she'd sparkle, and even the sparkle didn't have anything to do with the script. Kazan said, 'She's got the kind of beauty that's like royalty but it can get her into hot water.'"

Dekker told me, "Well, I had to press on that and I said what do you mean by 'hot water'? I just wasn't making a connection with that, and he said, 'well, you just said it, Al.' She had a wildness in her character, is what he meant. Not a wildness in a

Albert Dekker

Elia Kazan and Arthur Miller

negative sense, and then he went on to describe that it was all tied in with her inner sense, as he phrased it. She was this gorgeous deer that you spot on the side of a road at night and you catch her in your headlights. The doe's eyes flash wild and she jumps and is gone. It was that sense of the primitive, Kazan said, and we agreed it was connected to an eternal or unending motion of nature... I thought, that's one hell of a line to lay on a pretty girl and she'll sure as hell melt over that. But he was right. He had that instinctive way of getting at one's inner being and he'd presented an overall accurate description. He'd put into words something that was quite essential about Marilyn's character. It was the same, you see, that was in Jimmy Dean, the same similar contrariness that you couldn't pin down... Oh, he loathed Jimmy. He hated him as a person, as an individual, that is. Loved him to death as Cal in *Eden,* but off the set he detested him. It was Jimmy's deliberate self-indulgence Gadge (Kazan) hated. But here we had the reverse of that, with Marilyn. Her self-indulgence was so far from deliberate it wasn't even self-indulgence...

"It tickled me, as Harmon, who was happy as a clam to have Kazan on the set, the three of them going off, Kazan and Harmon and Marilyn, who even at lunch was hesitant and confused over Kazan's interest in her but all flushed at the same time like she had ants in her pants..."

Dekker said, "A couple years later we made *Eden* and we'd sit and talk at times, but apart from what I'd heard, and of course that was second-hand, Kazan was reluctant to talk about Marilyn because by then she was hooked up with Arthur Miller and there was all the awful business with the House Un-American Activities and Kazan being low man on that totem pole, and frankly he assumed she'd have nothing good to say about him. But we did talk about her one afternoon, just off to the side while we were doing that gymnasium scene, and something came up with to do with Monty Woolley being ill or in the hospital in New York...

"He'd mentioned cutting a scene, and brought up Harmon's directing—having gone from a superb editor, one of the best in the business, to directing which ultimately proved his downfall, and I mentioned Harmon having had some rough moments with Marilyn in that silly picture, though she came off well, and Kazan got immediately annoyed. He said he could sym-

119

With Joe "Palooka" Kirkwood, Jr.

pathize with Harmon's concerns, since Marilyn's personality would always transcend the screen. Stick out like a sore thumb, he said. He mentioned a patina that had to seal over a picture so that nothing, or and he stressed, '*no* one' meaning Dean as well, would appear to be climbing out of the picture like a trombone blast in the middle of a string concerto. He said well, that's what Marilyn is, a trombone blast and now she's a high-flying star and it didn't matter. I asked if he'd ever do a picture with her, and he said, 'Oh, god, no! I would never do a picture with Marilyn. She's far, far too undependable and lost in her own world,' and he said, 'like him,' and he meant Dean."

I met Constance Bennett in New York in the late '50s, and she became instrumental in my chasing down the halls of a serious acting career. She connected me with Josh Logan, a new agent, and with Jerry Wald. We talked about Marilyn and Miss Bennett, who'd worked in *As Young as you Feel*, said Kazan had, in fact, told Marilyn he was interested in using her in a picture, "For poor Marilyn," Bennett said, "striving to be a fine actress, this was like offering sweets to a honey bear."

She said Kazan was "immediately smitten" with Marilyn, and Marilyn was thrilled to death with his attention and interest in putting her in a Kazan picture. She told me he read with her—the script we had, and he could envision using her in an upcoming project. He went as far as to describe a part to her. So Marilyn went off with him believing he would use her in whatever movie he had in mind." Bennet said she was not so surprised that Kazan had told her that in order to guarantee the results he was after.

According to Jean Howard, actress, photographer, ex-Ziegfeld girl and ex-wife of producer and agent Charles Feldman (though Howard and Feldman still shared the same Coldwater Canyon house), "Kazan kept Marilyn on the string, but in time," she said, "she began to get sticky—that's what Kazan said, and he had to shake her off."

I later wrote a movie script based on a property owned by Charles Feldman, to be directed by Jerry Wald's associate, filmmaker Curtis Harrington, also co-producing with Jean Howard. The attorney representing our deal was the famed Fox executive legal advisor, Harry Sokolov.

During a meeting at the Coldwater Canyon house, Jean told me sarcastical-

ly, "Kazan was actively on the scene getting what he could from the usual young, starstruck girls that pour in from Idaho and Wichita Falls and the like." She said he brought Marilyn into his orbit with the usual spiel about putting her in a movie "in development" that offered a pretty young actress the possibility of being jockeyed to stardom. He brought Marilyn to the house on several occasions, Jean said, and they stayed together—"sleeping together—as well as being actively involved in our parties. He was supposedly on business and not with his wife, Molly, and his children. They were in New York. He made a habit of philandering and I personally did not approve to a great extent but Kazan's closeness was with my husband, Charles. They had *Streetcar Named Desire* in the works and Kazan was not especially close to me. He cheated on his wife endlessly and I imagine she looked the other way. The young girls Kazan hopped in and out of bed with came and went, and were of no more interest or retained by Elia than what he'd had for dinner the previous night or farted out after breakfast. With Marilyn he found a personality that was, as he would say repeatedly, 'a unique young woman...'"

Marilyn believed Kazan's desire to spend time with her, Jean said, forecast a greater involvement that he had in mind.

"I have to be honest and say my personal feeling about Marilyn is that the uniqueness was basically that she was hopelessly self-interested. An absent-minded manipulator—if there is such a thing. This is from my first-hand knowledge from the parties Charles and I gave which were close to prima facie events. My feeling is based on the time before Marilyn became one of the biggest stars in town, and then she didn't come out of her hiding. The poor girl was terrified since she had achieved what she was after and frankly it seems to me she was too ill-equipped mentally and emotionally to handle the success she'd achieved... She was someone who had absolutely no interest in another person. Her interest began and ended with Marilyn Monroe, and she did whatever she could to arouse you to share that same interest."

I felt sorry for the once-beautiful Jean Howard, an ex-showgirl who was gradually losing her nose to cancer.

Hollywood Hypnotism

She often put the ends of a couple of her fingers against her upper lip, gently tapping them like she was thinking of what she was going to say to something you'd said, or like she didn't want to show her teeth when speaking. Marilyn had wonderful teeth. They sparkled. Agent Henry Willson said my teeth were too small. I'd have to consider having them made bigger with porcelain caps or else pulled out and replaced with a partial of bigger front teeth.

Also Marilyn had a habit of stretching her upper lip down a little as if to draw it under her front teeth, maybe not fully aware she was doing it. She would pull on her upper lip as she spoke, sort of tucking it against the edge of her front teeth, the tip of her tongue poking for it. I figured by accenting the length of her upper lip, it made her nose look smaller, but this sometimes caused her to lisp. Her nose was also great but she did have several unusual ideas about her appearance, which after all was the most important thing about Marilyn. But she really didn't have to do anything. She could just stand somewhere and magnetic waves seemed to radiate around her.

Under her contract to Fox, she'd been rushed through a series of movies with well-known household favorites like Fred Allen, Eddie Bracken, Ginger Rodgers, Claudette Colbert and a bunch of others like June Haver and Bill Lundigan, called "bread and butter" names or "old standbys" in the front office. The only shining face in the lot was Marilyn's as she sparkled through short scenes in a smorgasbord of low-grade pictures—"your average second features" or clearly forgettable films.

"It was never easy," Marilyn said. "Never a breeze, and I only saw it as learning my craft as an actress because I'd never had a chance to learn anything. I mean how I looked or how I even sounded. I never had a chance to do it for myself…to be who I was. People can't understand that…"

She stood in that alcove in Wynn Rocamora's home on Outpost Drive, jerking on the telephone cord. The occasion was an afternoon gathering not that long after I'd met Marilyn on Doheny where Marilyn wasn't living anymore. Rocamora wore a crown of stars for successful clients, plus younger would-be's like myself, and though he wasn't Marilyn's agent (I'd asked him earlier that day), he smiled and said, "I'm working on it."

I had to say I was impressed Marilyn remembered me. She didn't remember my name though, except to say, "I know you, you're the friend of John Hodiak's..." I said yes, and told her my name though I didn't know if it logged in—not because she'd forget things, but she had a way of fixing faces in her mind with some label she'd stick on that she didn't shake. So I was John Hodiak's friend, and she'd introduce me as "John Hodiak's friend..."

She was having trouble with the phone. "Every time I try to call," she said, "this fucking line is busy." Flustered and jerky, she said she should call the operator and have "the telephone company" interrupt the other call. I asked if she did that often and she said, "I have to because otherwise I'm not able to reach the person when you have to talk." She dialed the long distance operator again and asked to try the number. Waiting, she asked me if I'd seen John Hodiak lately.

I said yes. She said he was such an "admirable person," then she hung up the phone. "Still talking," she said, then stretched her upper lip practically under her front teeth. She was staring at me and her eyes were uneasy with whatever she was thinking. She kept fiddling with the telephone cord. A number of people were laughing in the other room and I got the feeling she was somehow hiding. Instead of staring back at her, unsure what to say, I said I wanted to congratulate her on the movies she'd been making. Her eyes got wide, her lip going up and she seemed to grit her teeth.

She did that gesture with her hand at her mouth. "They're terrible," she said. "You can't be serious." I asked what picture she was doing next—just trying to keep us moving, and she said, "Oh, shit, I don't know—I don't honestly have any idea why I'm doing what I'm doing and it doesn't look very good or substantial..."

I said, well, I thought she was great in what she'd done. I said I'd been out to Fox on *Let's Make it Legal* but I was too young for the part. "Wagner did it," I said. "Richard Sales said I was too young to be married to Barbara Bates—"

"That is baloney," Marilyn said. "That was the part *I* was supposed to have, you know, the one that Barbara Bates did. I tested for the goddamn role and they had me at *ward*robe! Richard Sales is an asshole." Her eyes flashed and she said, "What I did anyone could have put up some wallpaper and it could've been me." I said, well, I thought she was great anyway and the scenes she'd had just were so convincing I was hypnotized.

Still staring at me in that odd manner, her eyes still intense but easing, she pushed her upper lip lower. It was those times, she said, "like you have just said, that are most rewarding in what I'm doing..." when someone would say such a thing as I had just said—being "hypnotized..." She sighed and looked around, yanking a little on the phone cord and said she was doing so many she wasn't even sure what she was doing because it was so terrible. I said I didn't think it was terrible at all and she said, well, my friend John Hodiak would understand and "he would say they were terrible. He's probably saying they're so terrible he can't stand to see the movies."

I said I understood, but what I was saying was those moments I'd just mentioned as being hypnotized by were the ones that made it possible to do the other crap—certainly not that what she had done was remotely like crap.

"Oh, crap!" she said loudly. "It *is* crap!" A fattish man in a blue gabardine suit was coming toward us, smiling at Marilyn and she hushed herself as if addressing someone else, and said to me, "Thank you, and I appreciate that about being hypnotized, but are you saying hypnotized as if in some trance like a hypnotist is going to do to a person?"

"Well," I said, "if you want to look at it that way..." Feeling I'd blabbed my way into a corner, I said, "If not hypnotized, then captivat-

ed—maybe that's a better word. At least for me, I'm an actor who wants to do something worthwhile or like what you said about it."

"What did I say?" she asked.

"You said 'substantial,'" I said. "I know what you mean by that and it's like me wanting to play the Montgomery Clift part in *Red River*—" She loved that film, she said, she loved Howard Hawks, even though he was always 'getting mad' at her. She loved John Ford, she said. She loved *Stagecoach*, and I said, "Now that *does* hypnotize me—" She said she wanted "desperately" to do a picture with John Ford, and she'd even dreamed of doing something like *Pinky*.

"My hair is red in what I dreamt," she said. "It doesn't have to be black—" No, I said, it didn't have to be black. "When one is hypnotized by a movie," she said, "do you suppose it can open something as seeing into a person's self such as hypnotism is supposed to do?"

I said I imagined that could be true. "Like being in a kind of identity situation—"

"A what?" she asked, "How do you mean 'identity'?"

"Identifying with the character," I said. "Carrying it with you and making it a part of your life, even if maybe it's only a yearning—"

"For something better," she said. "What is the point of doing something if it is not going to get any better? It's like a person being sick in bed and nobody comes to bring you even some toast." Perhaps that's

true, I said, not exactly sure what she'd just said, and then she said, "I have to try this fucking number again." She turned to the phone and dialed for the long distance operator. I was looking at her shoulder and her neck. She got connected and I moved politely to the side.

The fat man's face was round and blank as a pie tin as he said her name a couple times like calling her away from the phone. I didn't know if he was waiting for the phone or for her. He smiled. I said I was a friend of John Hodiak's. He said,

At Farmers Market, Los Angeles

"Oh, is John here?" I shook my head.

We waited while Marilyn made her whispered, anxious monologue of a call, neither of us piecing together what she was saying. Finished, she said, "Fuck them. When someone is in doubt over something and they won't try to understand, you can say 'oh, fuck you.'" The fat guy kind of nodded, reaching his hand which she ignored. He whispered something and she nodded, then gave a little smile and dutifully started off towards a huddle that included Rocamora, Rory Calhoun and Jean Howard.

Marilyn glanced back at me. She said, "Excuse me," to the guy, and held out her hand. I took it and we shook hands. She said in a muted voice, "I'm glad you're a friend of John's because he needs friends so awfully much right now. I would be a better friend, you know, I just love him and I think it is terribly sad what they're doing to him at a time when he is so terribly sad."

I wondered if she was referring to Anne Baxter, one of Fox's big stars who didn't like Marilyn and who Marilyn didn't like since they'd worked together in *All About Eve*. I was about to ask her what "who was doing what to him," but the fat guy said, "Marilyn—" and muttered something else. She did something with her hand like a little backwards wave to me, like saying *ciao* and giving that Italian wave that was more of a come hither than a go yonder.

She won the Photoplay Award in early '53 as "Hollywood's Fastest Rising Star", and showed up for her award in a gold dress designed by Travilla. The neckline plunged so deep to her waist that Joan Crawford made it clear that Marilyn's attire was offensive. She detested the gaudy dress, no doubt equally detesting Marilyn, and told columnist Bob Tomas that it was an outrageous affront to finer sensibilities that Marilyn appeared as she had.

Rock Hudson laughed. He said, "Crawford is just jealous. She can be a bitch on six wheels... Marilyn's award was for the fastest rising *new* star and they didn't have one for the slowest fading one." I didn't agree with Hudson about Crawford, nor did I agree with Crawford about Marilyn, who remarked later that Hollywood had worked her too fast. "They rushed me from one picture into another," she said, "and it isn't a challenge to do the same thing over and over when I want to keep growing as a person and as an actress. They never ask me my opinion. They just tell me what time to show up for work..." Working under great pressure, there were times when Marilyn wasn't sure what picture she was making and problems kept cropping up.

The front office said, "She's bringing in the gold and we'll keep it pumping while the going's great."

Dance coach Jack Cole, who Marilyn believed was her friend, said, "She can be impossible at times because she just freezes up. We're in the midst of something and she won't understand what it is. Like she blanks out. Half the time she complains she's sick and in pain and there's delays and everyone's sitting around with their thumbs up their ass. Talk to her and she freezes up. She goes blank and you can't reach her. If you push her she just folds it up and gets sick and the shot's called off..." Jack said he loved Marilyn, loved part of working with her but there were times when it was "a sheer impossibility...you can't do this again and again and again....you want to go cut your throat...you want to cut *her* throat."

The problem was Natasha Lytess, Jack Cole said. Marilyn had enlisted her to be her personal coach, "to be her *mother*." Skilled in the old school dramatics, and a kind of personal armchair psychologist, Lytess had found a not-too-concealed hole in Marilyn's psyche and in a short time had slipped into Marilyn like fingers in a hand puppet.

"Am I your friend?" she'd ask. Marilyn would nod and no doubt pull down her upper lip. Lytess would say, "You trust me, don't you?"

Marilyn would say, "Yes..."

"You know that I would do anything for you, don't you? Do you know why I feel this way and would and will do anything in the world for you?"

"Because you care about me," Marilyn would say.

"It's more than care, Marilyn." Lytess liked to paint a picture of two souls bound in art, and according to the coach, Marilyn's response was that she'd longed for her soul to be bound with one who cared about what she thought and felt.

Lytess managed to convince Marilyn she was that one, and then planted herself in Marilyn's life as the coach who knew every nuance of Marilyn's "enormous talents," as the soul partner and substitute mother and father as well.

"She dries Marilyn's tears," Jack Cole said. "Whispers in her ear and makes a completed shoot practically impossible due to retakes. She has Marilyn hooked on the end of a line like a fish. She's attached herself to

Billy Travilla, costume designer

Marilyn and has her convinced that she needs nobody else. Except for Marilyn, no one wants Lytess on the set, especially who's directing the picture. Marilyn doesn't pay attention to the director who most of the time she thinks is some kind of ogre out to stifle her and to exploit her. So Marilyn needs the confidence of this adopted, so-called friend and advisor who is making everyone's life impossible... The most impossible being Marilyn's life as a performer and actress.

"Lytess instilled in Marilyn the tendency to reject what she's doing as mediocre and beneath her abilities, while at the same time guiding her through the dregs as she calls it, so that the outcome is that Marilyn's work is not all she can be—not whole as she'd be able to do on her own and without the meddling. It's like a Svengali kind of thing, and I believe it's really Lytess that's in front of the camera acting her heart out—only she's got Marilyn as the puppet...I think it's sad..."

"What we've got," said one producer, "is a frail personality you can't push without getting her too upset. When she's upset she won't function. If you force her she spooks. It's like dealing with a child who takes your criticism or instruction as meanness and she's liable to run away... She needs a psychiatrist on the set and not a master wand-waving character who's plainly using Marilyn for personal aggrandizement. I lay awake nights sometimes wondering what Marilyn could do it she wasn't under someone's thumb or spell or willpower, and if she could just be left to do what she wants to do, I think it would be original and sensational... But then, what the hell, it does come out that way, doesn't it?"

I stayed long enough at Rocamora's to watch Marilyn as she spoke, looking uncomfortable forming whatever she was saying, her eyes dart-

ing around. I waited for her jittery glance to catch me again but it didn't. Wishful thinking, I recall telling myself.

Two guys were crowding her like sawed stumps of trees, one a photographer and the other a British newspaper guy. The fat fellow who'd escorted her from the phone had cornered Rory.

Something about Marilyn struck me that day Hodiak introduced us. I didn't know what it was, and I stood chewing crackers and cheese and choking on caviar. Whatever I was feeling confused me, at worst depressed me. I wasn't satisfied with who I was or where I was or what I was doing. I was lost in myself and alone in a crowd, taking apart the self that I was with, monkeying with what I wanted to be. Then that closeness I felt with Marilyn was like our skins were gone. We were mirrors reflecting one another and it scared me. That's what it was.

Sure, I said, it was all in my head. I'd been with two gals a few years older than me and both stars in their own rights. There'd been no question of tossing romance between us and taking it while it was there. That was not what I conjured about Marilyn. I'd been a little blinded by her light and now we'd added a scene in a hall with a phone—a few lines of dialogue, a busy line when she wanted to talk. Standing around talking, I was actually feeling invisible except for the hors d'oeuvres I'd stuffed myself with. I was Claude Raines' *Invisible Man*, and you could see the stuff sliding into my stomach.

Could I say "wounded by the encounter?" I sensed so was she by some stumbled-out piece of truth or a kind of ancient energy abstracted from the immediate surroundings, the proximity showing me sort of inside myself as if looking askance, skin shaken off like you'd shake a rug. In that snatched flicker, a light had shined into an empty space in me. I flashed on a picture in my head of Marilyn's mother kicking and struggling as she pushed the baby into the world, same as my own mom unloaded me from her womb.

It ran all around in me but wasn't charged by sex or the hunger that seemed smeared all over the faces surrounding her. Wasn't something that could ever be answered physically even if it came to that. Maybe it was something that could never be answered in any way. A guru or a wise man would gaze at the wallflowered Hollywood hot-shot me and simply shake his head.

She wanted her fame more than anything in the world. It defined her. She'd sacrifice for that. She owned it—hers alone. No one could take it away. But there was something lost. I could see when she wasn't offering some practiced, postured gesture. Her eyes belied it.

I wasn't sure I wanted that fame. It didn't hold me. I wanted something else and though I didn't know what it was, I knew I was closer to it than she was. I sensed, too, that she wanted to get in touch with what was missing in her life. That's what was revealed in the magic mirror—a hollow, blank face blackened-in like a child's silhouette. I had to get out of there.

It didn't matter in Hollywood who fucked who or who didn't get fucked. The Arabs would say it was written. Astrologers saw it in planetary motion. That's what would stay, rooted like an oak, the fact that there wasn't any way to make the connection.

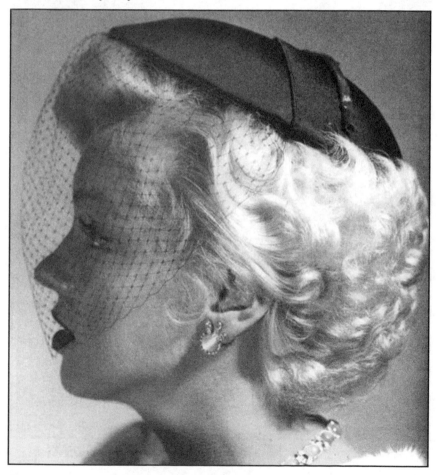

Un-American

A former associate of Elia Kazan said, "I broke off with him after he ratted to the House Un-American and sunk a lot of good people, including his pal, Arthur Miller, who had to scramble to keep himself from being imprisoned. I couldn't risk sticking close to Kazan and getting flak. I wasn't Kazan, and I had to drum up every job. The bigwigs were in favor of cleaning Communists and sympathizers out of the entertainment business and Kazan made himself a part of the *friendly* ones to the committee. Morally, I couldn't. A lot of people couldn't and wouldn't do it. They risked their necks, jobs—their families. The novelist Alvah Bessie, who wrote movies for Warner Bros., didn't name names like Kazan did, and he took the fall. Some of the most creative and brilliant writers in Hollywood were thrown out of the industry. They hid in Mexico to keep from persecution while Kazan got a pat on the head and kept making pictures."

Later, when Marilyn's name began to appear above the titles, Kazan underscored his "affair" with her, letting his "conquest" be indirectly known, though he claimed he tired of her "friendship." She had badgered him, he told John Stix in confidence, and he pawned her off to Arthur Miller. The ex-associate says, "Like ass-kissing Miller to try and ease his guilty conscience about having saved his own neck."

Arthur Miller was far from an urban lover boy and expressed great pleasure at the company of starlet Marilyn. Kazan had claimed he lacked the time to play nursemaid to someone who wasn't looking to "get laid for a part in a picture," he'd said, "but wants to be cradled like a fucking baby... Who the fuck's got the time for that?"

Miller believed he could make the time. Tall, gangly, a darling of the New York theater, he danced with Marilyn at Charlie Feldman's party, then took her for a drive along Mulholland Canyon.

Marilyn later told Susan Strasberg, "We looked at the lights and he told me about New York and how it looked when you were seeing down on the city...and Broadway. He held my hand and looked at my fingers, and said I had long fingers. 'I do?' I said, and then he kissed my hand

and we drove back to the Feldmans."

That same year, Marilyn's six-month contract with Fox was converted to a year deal. The grind began, one picture flowing into the next. Small, flashy parts until the following year when she was set for the lead in *Don't Bother to Knock*.

Natasha had landed a contract through Marilyn, to coach her through each "day of agony," as directors and other actors called working with Marilyn.

Some said it would get better as she gained more experience, but in truth it almost seemed with increasing work Marilyn's "phobias," as Zanuck called them, were getting worse. But the pictures were earning their keep and Zanuck was determined to "squeeze every potential dime out of that wiggling jello ass."

Marilyn would lose track at moments—unsure what she was doing, unsure of how to get where she was going. Before those around her noticed, she had someone to remind her, to guide her through the woods. Natasha understood Marilyn's need to be protected, guided and instructed, as though she stood teetering on the edge of a precipice, reaching away from a childhood of abandonment where her mouth was slapped shut and she had to padlock her feelings, showing only a clammed-up persona.

Modeling had been different. She'd smile and flirt or chase butterflies through roll after roll of film without once showing a shred of the interior.

As an actress, she could deliver little of this interior, nor could it be conveyed through any means, whether Richard Boleslavsky, Stanislavski's Method Acting, psychiatric counseling or just being a glamour puss. It was a carefully strutted persona she'd deliver to the merciless eye of the movie camera.

Even in conversation, Marilyn tended to offer a manipulated personality. It was like she was protecting some inner being, as though a separate self dwelled beneath her skin.

She studied scripts, memorizing lines as best she could, displaying sufficient involvement at certain moments. Natasha gave her line-readings which Marilyn half the time hopelessly memorized. For her, acting was really play-acting—a devised, ingenious, confidential method to deliver not only a convincing performance but one that seemed to shimmer on the movie screen. This quickly became the "acting" image Marilyn fitted over the actual Marilyn as if drawing herself into a skintight suit, and beneath this she hoped to remain guarded and unexposed.

Marilyn was loaned out to RKO for *Clash by Night*, a film to be directed by Fritz Lang. Featured with Marilyn was Keith Andes, who told me, "Here was a pinup cutie everyone was getting nuts about. The studio had a box office back-up because men wanted to see Marilyn's tits and her ass, and the women would go to get annoyed with seeing what they haven't got...

"When this picture was released, it was the same time that the nude calendar of Marilyn was out in the world. We were on the set in Monterey, and Marilyn and I were talking about the rough road getting into pictures. At least it had been tough for me, and she told me that because of things she'd done—referring to the nude calendar and hinting at other things, she said the studio was going to keep her under their thumbs, so to speak, and she would have to do their bidding. She said they told her in so many words, so she wouldn't have the opportunity of exercising any loopholes.

With Keith Andes, in Clash By Night

"The contract she had with Fox, which she told me about, was tantamount to a stranglehold, and she asked what could she do? I didn't know. I said talk to her lawyer or her agent, but then she said she could run away. I said, 'Run away? What are you talking about?' They'd have to find her, she said, but she'd hide, and soon as they found her—they'd have spies looking for her is what she said—they would sue her but she didn't have any money because of the contract. She said if she didn't have any money, which she said she didn't have, what then were they

going to do—shoot her?

"I guess I said, 'Marilyn, for Christ's sake, what are you talking about?' She just clammed up at that, wouldn't say any more. But she was right, this fuzzy, blonde bunny that had all these conflicts going on. She called it right because the studio tried to shoot her legally—to punish her. She outfoxed them, though, and each subsequent time she outfoxed them she became more important to the industry. No one was going to argue with the grosses tallying up because of Marilyn, and she knew it. She had it in her mind, which incidentally wasn't any empty-headedness by a long shot, that she was going to get *their* butts over the barrel for a change. 'Ring their gongs,' is what she said."

Marilyn's performance in *Don't Bother to Knock*, an intense, dramatic role, turned her head from the blonde bimbos bouncing in and out of scenes. "She wasn't getting the energy out of herself," said Ann Bancroft, who was making her debut in films. "Marilyn was using this application of what to do that was suggested by that coach. I wanted so desperately at moments to shake Marilyn like she was all wet and shaking this water off her, this application of what to do and what to say and how to frown or look scared or that sort of thing, and say to her, 'just let yourself *go*, Marilyn, just go inside yourself and let it go...'

"When she did it was a dream, so pure and truthful. She made me cry in the last scene in *Don't Bother to Knock*, and I wasn't crying in character. I was crying right in the scene because of what Marilyn was doing. The talent inside that girl was unquestionable, but it had to get out...For that scene there was some disagreement between Roy Baker and Marilyn and her coach—that Lytess woman. Marilyn ignored both of them. She did it her way and this got right inside me, actually floored me emotionally."

Richard Widmark initially believed it was "inconceivable that this gorgeous blonde is a fruitcake." Despite Marilyn's obvious abilities at carrying the role, Widmark told me he didn't like working with Marilyn because he couldn't relate to her as he did with so many actors during his long career. He brought up Barbara Bel Geddes in *Panic in the Streets*. He said he felt fitted into the role and could carry himself into the part, but with Marilyn, he said he couldn't. It was one of the most difficult pictures he'd made because he felt like he didn't have anything to do, and Marilyn was "all by herself," he said. "She wasn't shooting a scene with you, you were like participating in a scene with her, like you were a prop of some kind, and as though this was a stretched-out screen test for Miss Monroe. She wasn't involved with the other actors off or on camera."

Despite Marilyn's sense of fulfillment, Zanuck wasn't impressed with the picture. It wasn't making money, and he was convinced it was because of Marilyn playing something other than "her god-given gift at being a dumb blonde." Behind closed doors it was no secret that Zanuck thought Marilyn was cheap and wouldn't carry her weight. He said, "She's a dumb tomato and half-crazy to boot ... She's a sexpot who wiggles and walks and breathes sex, and each picture she's in she'll earn her keep, but no more *dramatic* roles!"

Apart from the sex-symbol jokes "they all" laughed about, says Lee Wallace, who later moved to head of casting at Fox, "what they enjoyed sharing," he says, "was the opinion that Marilyn was not only stupid, but incapable of emotion. 'She's empty as a paper cup,' said Zanuck. 'She wants to be a serious actress? I'm told she can hardly flush a *toilet* on her own, let alone find her way to the studio.'"

The next three pictures, Marilyn paraded and bounced and wiggled and grew more resentful, more determined every day, and more desperate to be carrying herself into something *serious*.

Her stock climbed despite Zanuck's displeasure at having her under contract once again. He vowed she'd never be cast in a role that demanded "intelligence and talent," because she lacked both, or had it all fucked out of her. That was the reason, Zanuck claimed, she'd been dropped by Fox the first time. "So she got goosed to Columbia, made a picture and *they* dropped her. We're giving her another chance, and let's hope she's not going to bite the hand that's feeding her."

Thousands of fan raves arrived weekly, yet Zanuck resented paying her an increase as called for. He said, "I'll pat her head, though everyone's patting her ass, right?"

Looking back at how they were handling Marilyn, Montgomery Clift said, "Fox wanted to keep a tight grip on her and drain her dry. That's what they were after. The best talents—the other artists, they saw that differently and understood Marilyn had a right to make that choice of not demeaning herself. But the boss wouldn't let her. They didn't want an actress. That's what they agreed upon. They'd sit at their fucking round table and decide that Marilyn wasn't capable of making a relevant decision."

"They had it in their heads that she's a bimbo," says Wallace. "Funny with comic dialogue if she can remember the lines, and on top of it—according to Zanuck's notion—she was '*tart*.' He said no way a tart can carry a picture with the support of the American public. He was saying stick her in a tragic role someday and you'd have to kill her off because nobody's marrying a tart and walking her off into the sunset."

Marilyn's fan mail was in the thousands weekly. She was a budding star, a promising, vibrant personality, but Fox decided to look the other way, pay her low, get all they could out of her before, as Zanuck predicted, "she starts herself thinking she's too hot for her britches..."

A year later, Marilyn's magic flared across the screen in *Niagara*. Joseph Cotton, starring with Marilyn, told actor Richard Allan, "She's like a damned atomic bomb... I only wish I could make better contact with her, and I don't mean that in an unsavory way. Everything she does is so remarkable on the screen, yet while you're shooting a scene, it's like there's a fog between you. It's an unsettling experience..."

Marilyn played Joseph Cotton's wife, taking a dark-haired lover on the side—played by Richard Allan. He wasn't a stranger to me; I'd known Allan since the year before. Marilyn took to Richard quickly, as she'd later do with Montgomery Clift, both sensitive men declaring a kind of secret simpatico with Marilyn—siding with her against the adverse powers she professed to be surrounding her.

"She experienced being an actress more as a kind of personal pain,

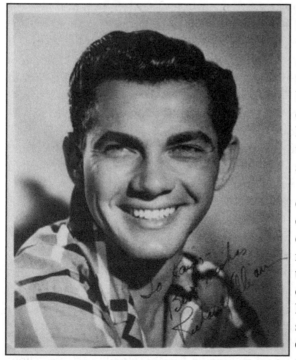

Richard Allan

some kind of disemboweling of her," Clift would say. "It was just about everything in the world she wanted, believe me, yet it emptied her and left her a nerve as raw as when the dentist drills away at a tooth."

Clift drank and downed pills to stay endlessly numb. He confessed, "Staying numb, you don't feel the pain. Living without the numbness is like living without any skin on your body and everything you encounter causes pain."

143

Marilyn understood. She stayed close to Allan during the *Niagara* shoot. He said, "She could bitch to me because she knew I cared about how she felt. I cared about what was troubling her. We talked about psychoanalysis and probing into the psyche. 'All I have to offer,' she said, 'is the actress that I am...'"

Gracious with fans to the point of over-extending herself, Marilyn would try to please those who showed awe. She'd pose for pictures and sign autographs until she ached. Her health was never that great. She bruised easily, continually fought colds and flu and developed a dread of bacteria. Allan said, "She'd wash her hands with Listerine and wore cotton gloves to avoid touching things."

Seeking to have his picture taken with Marilyn was a chubby, round-faced, sweaty man wearing obnoxious cologne. "Having worked for some rube paper," said Allan, "this guy claimed he was doing some Hollywood press like something for the *Hollywood Citizen News*. He was gewgaw over Marilyn since he'd seen *Asphalt Jungle*. This guy who said his name was Bob Slatzer hounded the *Niagara* set that day like a vulture. He got his picture taken with Marilyn, imposed himself on her—and on me, got me in a picture with him, and kept snooping for personal tidbits about Marilyn. I didn't like him—a guy if he borrowed your car you'd never see it again. Marilyn said, 'He keeps asking questions and I don't want to be rude...' I told her, 'Be rude. Tell him to take a canoe down the Falls.' She laughed... Henry Hathaway, directing *Niagara*, heard her laugh and said, '*That's* the laugh, Marilyn! Laugh like that when you laugh.' That made her laugh again.

"She was interested in astrology," Allan said. "A girl was doing charts—one of the cast, and she made a comparison between Marilyn and myself, saying we were astrologically brother and sister...

"That Slatzer guy never saw Marilyn again as far as I knew, as far as Marilyn knew and as far as anyone else in Hollywood ever knew..." Richard said, "The guy started running around claiming they'd been lovers even before Marilyn *got* into pictures—years before he ever showed up on the set that day... He sent sneak messages to the columnists, trying to get his name linked with Marilyn. Then he later made claims of having shared some long relationship with her when in fact no one in Hollywood had ever *heard* of the guy. He was living in another world. A nut! He never even *knew* Marilyn. But it hurt her, that character and others going around making up totally ridiculous stories about her. Poor Marilyn just couldn't understand why they were doing it..."

After *Niagara*, Marilyn phoned Richard many times. He said, "She told me our spirits *were* in fact linked in a 'sibling soul manner,' she said, something we could never comprehend because we're only 'small human beings.'

During *Niagara*, Marilyn told Richard that she had no friends. She had her coach, Natasha, at her elbow, working night and day with Marilyn, perfecting the outward appearance Marilyn was after, and a gamut of responses to suit the needs of a script. A fine-tuning application, shaping an external identity for Marilyn to adopt when in front of the movie camera. Marilyn's innate cleverness in perfecting the outward façade of a personality allowed few clues to her real identity to be revealed. Conflicts arose when what was brewing in that bottomless interior jarred with her surface performance. The result was often chaos. Fortunately, she had a good grip on the lid she kept secretly screwed tight.

"I saw the trouble coming," Richard said. "So alone she was, yet afraid to be alone. She said it was a prison and she wanted to know how to get out of it, to be set free. One night I could barely make out what she was saying. She'd been drinking and said I made her laugh. She said, 'Richard, I have to tell you no one in my life has ever loved me ... the person inside this terrible prison.' She said, 'I'm being abused, you know, and tortured by these people who won't love me ...' She said we should run away together—'far, far, far away,' she said, and we can be happy. She said, 'We can laugh about things...'"

Richard said he accompanied Marilyn to a secluded beach north of Malibu late one afternoon. "The sun was going down," he said, and she stared at the sun on the water, how it sparkled and flashed, and she talked about drowning—how the writer Virginia Wolfe filled her fishing boots with rocks and walked out into the ocean. She asked me if there was much pain to drowning..." Richard said he didn't know. She told him, "Perhaps it is possible that one doesn't have any pain that way because you suffocate, and as soon as you die your spirit can come above and be a part of the way the sunlight is on the water..."

Blondes Prefer Pills

On Marilyn's birthday in June of '53, she was told she would be starring with Jane Russell in *Gentlemen Prefer Blondes,* the role originally slated for Betty Grable. As Marilyn had proved a sleeper star, the brass decided to phase out Grable—who was "getting along," and pump higher octane into Monroe. Zanuck was pleased. He knew Marilyn would be sensational in the quintessential dumb blonde role, and he knew they'd be running crotch-high in profits. He was so pleased he bought a new limousine with the largest humidor available and a pull-down urinal he said was like a miniature Murphy bed.

When told of the Fox decision, Marilyn later said she felt her "stomach drop…" She got dizzy and scared, yet with somehow a safe feeling.

Years later I was talking to Jane Russell about her doing one of two dramatic roles in a Jean Howard and Curtis Harrington movie which I had scripted. I said it would've been fitting for Marilyn to have appeared with Jane in the picture, and we discussed Marilyn's relentless craving for a serious role and to be taken seriously. Jane said, "She could have done it wonderfully. When we worked together, I wanted to keep my arm around her and make her feel okay because that's what she needed, someone to tell her everything's okay and you're doing great. She had that, of course, from her coaches, but it was really important for her to have that same validation from those she was working with. Marilyn was sensational, and frankly I was more than happy to let her take the bows. She was so radiant and good she stunned you. No mater how long things took or the delays or problems in getting it, when she did it, she stunned you. She was so incredible you just stood there with your mouth hanging open.

"That spring we went to Grauman's Chinese, invited to put our hand prints and inscriptions into the cement, and I'll never forget her saying to me, 'This is for all time, isn't it?' Yes, I told her, it's for all time or as long as the cement lasts. She was so thrilled she was beside herself and she told me how she'd come to come to Grauman's when she was a kid and looked at the prints of everyone, and how she dreamed about being a movie star more than anything. It was something precious to me, her saying that."

Marilyn looked at Jane as they sank their hands into the wet concrete and as the camera flashed, she said, "Am I dreaming? Am I awake? This moment is out of the heavens to be a true thing happening." Jane says, "She made me cry, she was so sweet... I believed in her. We made a hell of a team and I wish we had done another picture together."

Fox followed *Gentleman Prefer Blondes* with another dumb blonde role for Marilyn. Rory Calhoun made three pictures with Marilyn, and said, "After *Ticket to Tomahawk*, the second one was *How To Marry A Millionaire,* followed by *River of No Return,* which wasn't a comedy. It gave Marilyn a chance to spread her wings a little as an actress. At first, I was happy as a peach to work with Jean Negulesco—one of the best directors in the business, who was doing *How to Marry a Millionaire.* I was playing lover boy to Betty Grable and not to Marilyn, and I would marry Grable in the picture. My working with Marilyn was limited due to the story, though we'd known one another since we'd worked in *Tomahawk.* Back then she'd had a small role but stood right out... I saw in the second picture how she was getting the kid gloves handling. Negulesco treated her with a respect that made her feel okay. That's what it was—she had to feel like she was somebody important, and was usually worried, or was scared, and she'd get difficult and it was pretty hard to stick to what you wanted. We did scenes and she'd freeze

right up—couldn't separate herself from the camera being right there...

"She talked a little about when she was a kid and being scared of things—of people, and I'd sure as hell had no easy time as a kid myself. We had something, a kind of chemistry I think that hooked up and I tried to make her feel comfortable. But the fact was, she didn't have the confidence back then to really know what she was doing. She was distant because she had all these props—I don't mean movie props, but personal ones, the special treatment angle... What the hell, she was very sensitive and hungry for someone to take charge in a decent way, and as an actress, being funny as hell, you couldn't watch anyone else, not even Betty Grable. It was almost impossible for anyone in the shoot and the crew, too, not to bust out laughing with what she'd do in a take, she was so damned funny. Man, she had the ability and all she needed was to gain the confidence...

"Marilyn's coach Natasha kept insisting on take after take, and Jean Negulesco didn't care about that, he was aiming to please and get the best possible picture he could out of Marilyn. He seemed to know exactly how to play his cards, and I have to say he was one of the finest directors I've had the pleasure of working with. He said whatever it took, he didn't want Marilyn to go bananas on him. Her security blanket was Natasha, he said, so what the hell. We had a ball."

Negulesco later said, "I knew Natasha Lytess was feeding on Marilyn's insecurities and pulling in a hefty salary as a result of that. I figured, okay, we'll let it ride because *I* wasn't paying Natasha and as long as Marilyn felt secure, that's what was important. Marilyn was carrying the picture. Bacall and Miss Grable were decorations."

During the making of *Shock Treatment*, Lauren Bacall told me Marilyn did not look at her acting partner during scenes, but was "looking past as if staring at someone behind you. Eye contact threw her off. She'd forget whatever she was supposed to say if another actor was looking directly at her. That was terribly disconcerting to deliver lines to someone who isn't focused on you but is staring into some god-knows-where space. I thought, holy *cow*, how am going to *deal* with this?"

"It could be seen on the set," Rory said. "What you saw, you'd wonder if it was any good. It looked *off* at times, like it wasn't part of the scene, but then you saw it on the screen and you had to admit the girl was on target even if nobody else knew what the hell she was doing half the time."

Bacall and Grable dealt with it. They teamed up to help Marilyn. Grable knew what was happening: Marilyn was heading into the top spot at Fox while Grable was on her way out, even with five years remaining on her contract—which she tore up later, saying, "Hey, I've had enough."

When *How to Marry a Millionaire* finished shooting, Bacall says she told Marilyn, "'It has been a real pleasure working with you and I want to say I admire you.' That's what I told her and she hugged me. I said, 'You've got what it takes, kid. You've got a future ahead of you that is roses, and you'll be able to do your best work when those jokers up front get their noses out of their assholes.'"

Marilyn was glowing from the compliments, recalled Ralph Roberts. "It meant a great deal to Marilyn that those two major stars appreciated working with her."

But Marilyn's magic was all but denied by director Otto Preminger. Rory said *River of No Return* was "a horse of a different hue." A dramatic film, none of Marilyn's comedic streaks were summoned and Preminger demanded his cast, according to Rory, "be on tap like a faucet. He controlled the picture like a dictator and let it be known he had no time to spend with the talent, only that they follow his direction and do what he'd tell you. So what happens with someone like Robert Mitchum in the movie, he just does all his Robert Mitchum things and pretty much walks through the movie. Preminger liked Mitchum but he didn't like Marilyn. I have to say neither did Mitchum like her. He was resentful and disrespectful, and in one scene where he almost rapes her, she's running away and he grabs her, knocks her down. He actually hurt Marilyn and I was surprised. She was lying on the ground in pain, but Mitchum didn't even help her up. They just walked away out of the scene—him and Preminger, who'd had no patience with her. He treated Marilyn and myself, and the rest of us for that matter, in an unwelcome manner. He never let up on Marilyn. I said once, 'She's trying the best she can and she needs help and encouragement, and needs to know what she's doing is okay.' He didn't like that. He just looked like me like 'who the fuck are you?' and he didn't treat her any different. A great director but a prick as a human being. That kind of crap makes you sometimes just want to walk away from the business.

"Marilyn did not do the best she could have done—neither did Mitchum nor myself, though Preminger pretty much ignored me. I think we all stunk and I think the picture stunk because Preminger wouldn't give us an inch. 'Know what you are doing!' he kept saying, yelling like we were a bunch of dinks off a boat. Marilyn hated the final cut and I had to agree. By then she was pissed at Fox and she said she felt like she was being run through a meat grinder."

Marilyn's next picture, *There's No Business Like Show Business,* proved harrowing for director Walter Lang. Later, when asked about Marilyn, he'd usually shake his head and say, "Don't ask unless you got hours to listen to misery…"

Half the time, Lang said, "Marilyn complained that she was sick, and this went on all summer. She complained of bronchitis and said she was anemic. She'd gain weight and she'd lose weight. She'd look bloated at moments and say something was wrong. She was on pills for aches and pills for nerves and pills for whatever. I think she was having serious side effects from these medications, and she'd be drinking on top of it and would appear groggy and lethargic. She'd be crying and destroyed if she was criticized, and she'd take some more pills to feel better…

"It was a *terrible* experience. There were days—*days* spent shooting around Marilyn because she couldn't make an appearance. Everyone was furious—fit to be tied. She wouldn't listen to me and I was directing the goddamn picture."

Eve Miller had a small part in the picture. I met Eve through actress Ann Savage at the Coffee Dan's on Hollywood Boulevard west of Cahuenga. I'd seen Eve in *The Big Trees* with Kirk Douglas, and though she'd had only a bit part in *No Business Like Show Business*, she'd talked to Marilyn "a little," she said, "because Marilyn seemed to single me out as someone to talk to off on the sidelines—someone who didn't have an ax to grind against her. I admired her and she was aware of that." Eve said she was surprised Marilyn decided to talk to her, remote as she seemed to most of the others except Donald O'Connor. Eve said she knew O'Connor herself from another picture but it had been a while. Eve told me she'd been under contract to Fox years before.

"Marilyn knew I'd done a picture with Kirk Douglas," she said, "and we talked about him and Billy Wilder. She told me she would have loved the role Jan Sterling had in Wilder's *Ace in the Hole*, which Kirk

Douglas had starred in as well. I thought Marilyn might've been a little too pretty for the Jan Sterling part, which was before Jan had a nose job. Marilyn said she thought the operation had ruined Jan's career. She said, 'It wasn't her idea, you know...' Jan was married to Paul Douglas who Marilyn said was a good actor but very cross and nasty with Marilyn when they made *Clash by Night*. She said, 'I don't want to work with him again even though people say he's such a nice guy and all that.' She'd crossed paths with Paul  Douglas at Fox when they made *Let's Make it Legal*, but Marilyn didn't think they could be very friendly because of what an astrologer had told her. She said she didn't know whether to believe the astrologer or not, but Marilyn said, 'I'm a Gemini,' and asked when my birthday was."

Later, Eve says, "Marilyn brought me a cup of coffee and she was reading a typed copy like a manuscript that was held in a notebook. I thought it was another script and asked if that's what it was, but she said it wasn't a script. The title was about labor in the transition from ape to man—something like that, and Marilyn said it was from a book by Friedrich Engels, the co-author of the *Communist Manifesto* with Karl Marx.

"I said, oh, my god, if anyone catches you reading that they'll think you're a communist. She looked at me very innocently and asked, 'Oh, do you think so?' I said yes, certainly everybody was talking about communists, and especially in the movies. She said she read a lot—poetry and philosophy, and what she had was given to her to read, I think she said 'Michael' had given it to her. But since I was uncomfortable and worried about it, she put it away in a little suitcase bag she had that had a lot of stuff in it — papers and hair curlers, and a bag of peanut brittle...

"She gave me some peanut brittle and wanted to take time to talk but she was really on call every minute, and there were all kinds of problems. It was terrible and I felt really badly for Marilyn because I could see she was asserting herself but there was just so much resistance against it... Then she was off by herself, complaining that she was getting sick, or she was with her coach, Natasha, who was reading lines over and over to Marilyn, putting inflections on certain words. She was giving Marilyn line readings, and then she'd hug her afterwards. Always seemed to hug her and then during a take she'd be almost directing Marilyn—and that was causing trouble. Marilyn wouldn't be looking at the person she was in the scene with, but looking past everyone to Natasha who'd be giving Marilyn some kind of signals...

"Once I heard Natasha say Marilyn's makeup was too heavy and coarsened Marilyn's features... An argument erupted, some disagreement over the makeup and Marilyn finally had the changes the way she wanted them, her eyebrows appearing lighter. There were a lot of problems on the set and it was pretty obvious that Marilyn was not happy doing the picture."

Eve said, "I enjoyed working in it, as short a time as I did, and the time Marilyn was talking to me. It caused me to wonder if she really cared or if it was that she wasn't hobnobbing with the other stars. I think Marilyn saw me as someone who'd had a hard time in the business, and I was trying to keep my head above the water. My feeling is that she saw something in common with me, something that rang true from the difficult experiences she'd had in her life, and wanted to share this and

possibly be friends. I couldn't see that she had any real friends associated with the pictures or once she was off the set, and I didn't know really if visiting with me was a gratuitous act on her part, like she felt sorry for me and at the same time was snubbing the important cast members by talking to me. Except for Donald O'Connor, they were annoyed with Marilyn's behavior, her lateness and how she felt. I don't know, but she gave me personal courage, even her interest in the forbidden communist writings was a sign of her not taking things at face value. She lifted my spirits more and that made me feel good...

"I believe she wanted to continue our friendship because she suggested I might want to accompany her driving up coast to Santa Barbara, but we never did. I gave her my phone number and address...

"I didn't hear from her until later in the year when she sent me a big box of dried fruit and nuts. I thought it was so sweet and her note saying, 'Thanks for being a friend...' It was so nice because I'd had a lot of problems the year after we made that picture, and things had gotten out of hand. Her gift came at an opportune time. I thought maybe she had heard about my having tried to kill myself and being in the hospital."

Curtis Harrington

Eve's boyfriend, a bit player at Universal, did not want to get married as quickly as Eve desired, so she had attempted suicide by stabbing herself in the stomach with a paring knife.

"After that," Eve says, "I didn't hear from her for more than a year and then she sent me a birthday card. I thought that was so considerate of her, to actually remember me, and to have remembered my birthday from when we'd talked about astrology."

After several discouraging years, Eve Miller succeeded in committing suicide in her Van Nuys apartment.

Producer Jerry Wald's associate, Curtis Harrington, says about *No Business Like Show Business*, "Marilyn *made* the picture. She *was* the picture. Who would see such a sophomoric, hackneyed movie if it wasn't for Marilyn? The cast was almost to the letter *brutally* miscast, except for numbers by Mitzi Gaynor and Donald O'Connor, and of course Marilyn. Otherwise the picture was a complete dud. The reviews were awful, and once again stressed Marilyn's character as the dumb blonde and she balked at that. She felt her career was an uphill battle, and which it basically was, her dealings with Fox. She'd been excited and effervescent in her moods, only to swing low to gloomy angers and voicing how she craved to do dramatic parts. She'd believed she was on her way—that *Don't Bother to Knock* and *Niagara* were affording her the kind of success she wanted. Well, she wasn't getting it... Instead she was becoming a joke and she resented that in no uncertain terms."

Richard Allan told me, "She said, 'We made a great movie, didn't we?' That's what she wanted—to do something important. She told me the kind of pictures she wanted to make and said everybody would want to see them because she *could* do it."   She was on her way, she told Allan. She was now a "big star" and had decided it was time she took charge of her life and career.

Producer Stan Rubin says, "That wasn't how the studio was viewing the situation. *They'd* make the decisions, they told her. Or should I say *warned* her? They made policy, not Marilyn. They laid it on her that her

contract was ironclad and Marilyn wasn't running the studio.

"I can remember Marilyn and myself walking on the lot and passing the windows of the top brass. Marilyn said to me, 'Someday I'm going to show those assholes that I can *act*! Even if I have to take things into my own hands.' That someday she was talking about was going to come real fast."

Breaking Away

Marilyn said no to another bimbo run through a picture. The studio laughed but Zanuck was getting red around the gills. "You'll do the picture," he said.

"I haven't even seen a script yet!" Marilyn complained.

"You don't have script approval," she was told. "Now don't be difficult at this point, Marilyn. We want you to do a picture, you do the picture. You're not in business for yourself, Marilyn. You're part of a team. The picture's made for you and we're bending over backwards—"

"They're fucking bending *no*where!" Marilyn told Milton Greene, a handsome young photographer who'd managed to corner her at a party. Greene suggested she walk out—tell them to shove the stupid movie, didn't matter if Frank Sinatra was doing it or not. Marilyn said, "I'm through playing somebody walking into tables and batting my eyes. I want to do something *meaning*ful."

"Meaningful *schmeaning*ful," Zanuck said. "We shoot the picture. Enough is enough."

No, it wasn't enough, Greene told her. He said it was ridiculous. She had star status—she'd carry a picture, he said. She wasn't going to do any more stupid roles but the studio said, oh yes, you are. She said "Oh no, I'm not, and you go fuck yourselves." She deserved the right to approve the scripts she was investing her life into.

"So what are you going to do?" Greene asked.

Marilyn said, "I can tell you what I'm *not* going to—"

And she didn't. She didn't show up for the first day's shooting on *Girl in the Pink Tights*. Zanuck said, "Who the fuck does she think she is? Why don't I just go home and go to sleep, right? Let *Miss Marilyn Monroe* run the fucking studio!" Then he said, "She's on suspension as of this minute."

Marilyn was scared, but excited. She was not available for comment. In fact, she wasn't even in Hollywood. She was getting married to Joe DiMaggio in San Francisco. It was mid-January '54 and cold. Natasha Lytess said, "She walked off without a word like she was run-

157

ning and hiding, and I didn't know exactly what she was up to. She was being extremely secretive." Natasha said she didn't like DiMaggio. She said she couldn't accept the *hombre* swaggering he concealed beneath a feigned kindliness that offset his "rampant conceit." Poor Marilyn, Natasha said. She'd found another father figure to try and wedge into that hollow, empty place in her heart. "Oh," Marilyn had said, "I do care so very much for Joe and he tells me how much he loves me almost on the half-hour of every hour..."

They were to have a honeymoon in Japan. Joe was grinning from ear to ear but the honeymoon was aborted when Marilyn accepted a USO tour of Korea. For four days in February she entertained over sixty thousand servicemen—many who had not seen Marilyn's movies, as they had been in the service during her rise to star status, though most had seen photos of her in magazines and newspapers. Marilyn said later, "It was one of the most happy moments in my life. As far I could see I was looking at thousands of young faces and they were all cheering me, and they were yelling and clapping, and standing in the snow. I was feeling that for the first time in my life I had no fear of anything, and I only felt happiness..."

DiMaggio didn't accompany her on the USO tour. He made it clear that he hated "crowds and glamour."

Ralph Roberts said, "It was difficult to be in contact with Marilyn as she was on the go every minute, not to mention that Joe didn't like the idea of her associates or anyone connected to the movies. He had it in his mind that Marilyn would walk away from her career and be wife to DiMaggio. That's what he wanted and in no uncertain terms. I don't know how Marilyn let herself get into that situation with a person so totally different than she was, other than the idea that he represented a pinch-hitter or backup strength for her... I don't believe she considered what he had in mind for her or the life he planned which definitely did not include her career, definitely did not include the movies or the Hollywood life which is all that Marilyn really knew..."

Natasha, nearly ignored by Marilyn after the wedding, said later that DiMaggio, for all his bravado, was essentially a weak man of mediocre character and concerns. "It was doomed from the start," Natasha said. "Anyone could see that... He wanted Marilyn as a flashy stickpin, to show off a conquest, that he was superior to us trivial show business people. But what he did was bite off more than he could chew and thus resorted to his more primitive self which included violence against Marilyn. She was a very frail and sickly girl though you would-n't know it. But she was, and DiMaggio hurt her physically..." Marilyn carried the bruises to show for it.

She had made *The Seven Year Itch* and it was during the sidewalk skirt blowing scene that DiMaggio freaked. He'd been called by Walter

Winchell and informed that his wife was exposing herself to a couple thousand onlookers in the middle of Times Square. "What're you gonna do about it, Joe?"

By October '54, after only eight months, Marilyn and DiMaggio were already separated. Shortly after that, Milton Greene had swooped Marilyn into the New York corporate world by instructing her in the formation of Marilyn Monroe Productions, of which Greene would be vice-president. The company would allow Marilyn to produce the kind of movies she sought to make.

The enterprise was small—Marilyn the president—but the plans were far-reaching. Greene said, "Marilyn wanted to make serious movies—good films, important films. She knew what she wanted. There was never a question of that or of the kind of integrity she sought to embrace."

Her walking out of the Fox contract had made a hole in the dike—a crack in the studio system. Casting director Lee Wallace says, "She was an operator, an innovator, and broke a hole in that otherwise impenetrable power structure. Things weren't going to be the same, and Marilyn had a lot of sympathy from the movie-going public. She made the studio bend favorably to her position. With *The Seven Year Itch* she'd shot to the position of the hottest movie star in the world."

Director and actor Frank Corsaro of Actors Studio says, "Marilyn's acquaintanceship with Arthur Miller had been ongoing for a number of years, but became intense that period in fifty-five when she entered Actors Studio and found support from the Strasbergs. I'd have to agree with Miller when he said she was completely unconventional, a most original human being. One of a kind...and bursting with promise and excitement for the arts..."

In March '55, "Marilyn rode a gigantic pink elephant in Madison Square Garden," says Ray Myers, actor. "The elephant was painted pink and it was a fund-raising benefit for arthritis. Marilyn was in like a can-can outfit... Only Marilyn would've done it, an important movie star getting on top of a huge elephant. She was like God in drag."

"Marilyn came to the Actors Studio with her heart in her hand," said actress Shelley Winters, "not like people wanting to show how talented they are. Not that Marilyn was like a stray or a lost soul, because she had an agenda that was pretty reasonable. She wanted to work—to study and

Shelley Winters

improve her craft, and she believed Lee (Strasberg) would be able to guide her. She wanted so badly to be connected to theater people, serious writers and performers. Naturally, Lee took Marilyn under his wing. I should say he did this more than happily because Marilyn being associated with Actors Studio was a big feather—I should say a *plume*, for Lee and Actors Studio...

"She was crying for help with that quiet urgency she'd mastered, and then projecting it as a life and death situation. Lee was taken aback but he quickly took her in. I think her unrestrained need to be saved in some way overwhelmed him."

Strasberg summoned Shelley to a private meeting. She said, "It was just Lee and myself, and he said, well, Marilyn was an important star in the world, and I believe in her enormous potential, and setting that aside he asked me to help her feel secure and to put her trust in Lee. He said 'We're her family now, Shelley, and you can be a true blue sister to Marilyn.' This was all right with me except it was peculiar for Lee to be saying, and the manner in which he said it, like he was involving me in some underhanded activity. But what he meant was that Marilyn was not in control of her own ambitions or kind of like he was saying her stability...

"I don't know that Marilyn saw it this way," Shelley said, "and she very often wasn't in accord with what you were thinking was going on with her... I mean, if you were scrutinizing the person. But okay, I did try to make her feel as comfortable as I could, not that she was *un*comfortable but like she described to me that she was on a crusade.

That's how she put it, a crusade to find the meaning of her own life that would give her the strength to succeed in being the true actress she wanted to be. She said 'true actress...' It was like she wanted to trade in who she had been and become someone else. The problem was she didn't know if she'd be granted the chance, and that was where Lee was intervening; having her invest her trust in him, believing he would be instrumental in the realization of her dreams. However, I didn't lay it on thick like that or try to butter Lee up in her eyes. That wasn't necessary. And she became very close to Susan Strasberg (Lee and Paula Strasberg's daughter), who was—you know, like a black sheep in her family, and Marilyn could latch onto that pretty easily, having been a black sheep all her life and even being in New York like she was—thumbing her nose at Hollywood."

The studio system, Shelley said, "hadn't wanted Marilyn to grasp the idea of her own freedom and volition, or the idea or concept of having a say. They wanted Marilyn the willing queen of the dumbbells to make them a lot of money. And she *did* shine. Just sitting still in the back of the room where she always sat, just sitting still like she'd do, and sort of leaning forward, listening so intently, and she seemed to glow, it was like a light was on her. There isn't any doubt that Marilyn was probably the most beautiful woman who has ever walked on the earth, and the rest of us just have to do the best we can, like God gave it all to her."

Meanwhile, the consensus of opinion at Fox was that Marilyn had "a rebellious, uncooperative personality," and her thinking wasn't well-balanced. "Her emotions," Zanuck said, "are those of a child. As wonderful as she appears on screen, she is ill-equipped to dictate terms, too young, too unsure of herself and too frightened."

"Marilyn's temperament," another producer said, "is such that she's incapable of responding in a businesslike manner."

Ralph Roberts said, "Marilyn wanted what was due her. She wasn't interested in taking over or bossing anyone. She wanted what she deserved—more money than the grip or hairdresser, which is what had been happening. She was smart to refuse to do any more of their bidding, and if they fired her, she said they'd want her back but she'd agree only under new terms..."

Shelley said when Marilyn became a fixture at Actors Studio, it was as though Lee singled her out, as though there was a move to save Marilyn and show her that her affiliation with Actors Studio was in fact the saving grace of her career and coincidentally her emotional security and her sanity. Shelley said, "Lee told me once that had he been instrumental in convincing James Dean to remain in New York a little longer, Jimmy wouldn't have died. But the problem, Lee suggested, was that Kazan wanted Dean for the Warner's movie *East of Eden*, and neither hell nor high water was going to deter him from realizing that. He even went out on a limb with Warner's, telling them that either Dean did the movie or they could hire another director.

"Though Kazan and Marilyn had been sociable for a while, and more than sociable, I have never understood why he didn't use her in something. He could have been so instrumental in moving her career forward but he didn't see her that way. After she made *Gentlemen Prefer Blondes* with Jane Russell, the occasion came up and I asked Kazan why he'd never used Marilyn and he said because she would have been a distraction. I said, a distraction? What was he talking about? You can't take your eyes off Marilyn and he said that was what he meant. She hadn't been right for a lead in anything he'd done so far and that said to me he had never intended on using her in a picture..."

Reluctantly, Shelley said, "He only used her—period, I'm sorry to say. And Hollywood was in the process of developing a star and claiming they'd invested a great deal into this effort. They could've been talking about an eggbeater."

Yet Strasberg realized that a goose capable of laying golden eggs wandered into his parlor seeking sanctuary. "Lee had instantly recognized the importance of Marilyn being fitted into Actors Studio. She was a light globe," Shelley said, "and we all basked in her glow..."

Half a century later, at a party in Beverly Hills which I attended with Kevin McCarthy, Shelley was in a wheelchair. She had suffered a stroke and it would be the last time we spoke. She kept her hand on my arm the entire time. She said, "I think about Marilyn a lot now and I wonder if there's a heaven if we'll be together. She had all the beauty that God could bestow but then He took it away. He let us live and He took Marilyn away... I loved Marilyn."

Washington Square in the Rain

Marilyn's big black sunglasses half-hid her face. A black scarf covered her hair and was tucked around her neck, and even the cab driver couldn't tell it was Marilyn Monroe he was carrying in his taxi. She wore slacks, sort of rumpled at the bottoms, Saks loafers, no socks on her feet. The forest-green raincoat looked too big. You couldn't see her hair or eyes or a hint of makeup. On her left was a young actor from Actors Studio, Ray Myers, someone tagging along to keep her company at the request of Lee Strasberg, because she had "trouble right now being by myself," as Ray told me. Doing stooge runs for Strasberg could steer you nearer to a membership at the Studio. Ray told the driver, "The lady wants to walk barefoot on the grass in Washington Square."

The cabbie said, "Which side of the square?"

Ray was a New Yorker, a pal of John Stix, one of the first directing members of Actors Studio, and Stix was also a friend of mine from a Broadway play he'd directed.

We had a bottle of champagne and a light, afternoon rain was hitting the taxi windshield as we reached the Village.

Ray and I flanked the incognito Marilyn as she strolled across the grass in Washington Square, rain like a fog around us. Ray carried her shoes while she kept her hands in the pockets of the baggy raincoat. I toted the champagne. We popped it open in the square, Marilyn sitting on a bench with her hands still hidden, saying how she wished we were listening to Vivaldi. She said Arthur Miller had looked her in the face and said, "Tell me what you know about Vivaldi."

Ray had picked up a pack of paper Dixie cups and as we shared the champagne, Marilyn blurted out, "I *know* about Vivaldi, for God's sake," then started to cry. Her eyes hidden behind the enormous glasses, the tears leaked down her cheeks, her mouth struggled to swallow the sobs. Ray put his hand on her shoulder and said to take deep breaths. She shrugged his hand off, saying, "I know how to breathe—" I smoked until it started raining harder and put out the cigarette. Marilyn

165

didn't budge from the bench, like she was unaware of the rain. We sat with her, saying nothing.

My jacket wasn't water repellent and I was getting soaked. I remember how much at that moment I wanted to be a part of Marilyn's life—didn't even know what part I wanted to be a part of. Some union had fused us, a kind of  recognition like one leper spotting another. You couldn't pin it on a bulletin board or get your brain around it, but I'd thought if we could leave our bodies, the part of us hanging in the air would congeal. I remember thinking all that as we sat dropping a couple pills and chasing them with the bubbly, goosing the caps straight to the brain.

Maybe, too, what I was feeling *was* the bodies—a physical thing. I was so drawn to that back then and yet I couldn't get across the wide moat of who she was—her success, that is—even though half the time she appeared so miserable you wanted to look the other way. But you couldn't. At least I couldn't, and neither could anyone I knew who was close to her or was agonizing through making a movie with her. It was that inner being I felt attached to, and no matter how awful she seemed sometimes, if she asked I could have thrown myself in front of a taxi, if that's what she wanted. Sounds wild now, irrational—some super romantic *black ship to hell* kind of thinking or just plain stupid.

All of us wet by then, Ray said to her, "Café Rienze's across the street. Maybe you'd like to get out of the rain?"

"No, I can't go anywhere," she said. She didn't want to leave the bench. Something about someone else might take it and we'd have to stand if we decided to come right back. Ray and I exchanged a look. Her thinking, he said later, was "a bunch of unrelated fragments..."

She'd made *The Seven Year Itch*, and DiMaggio accused her of obscene behavior, of enjoying it, like her "damn near bared crotch showing to half of New York..." He accused her of being an "exhibitionist" and said only a "whore at heart would pull such a stunt." They screamed and fought. He struck her.

"You know, I am very close to Joe," Marilyn would say during the brief marriage. "But we can be so very far apart it is like two ships in two different harbors." DiMaggio'd wanted a good Catholic wife and "gobs of squabs,"as Marlon Brando had put it in *On The Waterfront*.

To Marilyn, DiMaggio had reflected a caregiver who was capable of taking away the sadness she believed had penetrated her soul. She could pass her troubles to Joe and he'd take care of them. The only problem was that Marilyn found herself on a dead-end, one-way street. She told Susan Strasberg, "I had no way to love him because he didn't want me to be who I have to be..."

There was now desperation beneath everything she was doing, like she was creeping into some coming-apart of her nerves. In the park, she said, "Control is the most important thing, isn't it?" repeating another of Strasberg's lines as rain ran down the lens of her glasses. "A person's own life," she said, "belongs to them... If you don't want to think that it belongs to God, that is..." Her face turned toward me and she said, "Hodiak had a terrible time, didn't he?" He had died a month after James Dean was killed in the highway wreck. "Hodiak was a wonderful actor and he had a terrible, awful time," Marilyn said. "He was someone whose talent I cherish, and do you know what he was? He was like Robert Ryan in the way this business constantly overlooks the truly great talents that are right under their noses..."

I agreed with her.

Stix had said, "I don't know if she's done the right thing or not, walking out on her contract. She's still young and I don't know what she's doing or planning on doing with these production ideas. They're not clear and I confess I don't trust the situation she's involved in. One can easily see mistakes in things other people do...but I think she's made a costly choice and I don't know if it was the right one..."

Her head dropping as she sat on the bench, Marilyn made a face and said she was sick. "I think

Jonathan Gilmore, New York

I'm going to throw up," she said. "I don't want to vomit on the grass because people are liable to step in it ..." Ray said he'd get some paper towels from Rienze. No, she didn't need it, she said. She wasn't going to puke after all. She said, "All the time I feel like I have to throw up... but then I don't really have to. It's just how I am feeling." I couldn't see her eyes to tell if she was still crying but she kept blowing her nose.

Later that month, I was attending a small dinner party at John Stix's apartment. I'd been going over the Lee Strasberg tapes from the lectures he gave during sessions at the Studio, and since I'd written a quick novel, Stix had asked if I'd think about transcribing Strasberg's tapes. I'd always been making notes — a lot about memory and how we remember and what we remember.

Kim Stanley was at the little get-together, along with Maureen Stapleton who was going to bring Marilyn, but Marilyn was so late in getting ready, Maureen came on her own. Another young actor was there, a new member of the Studio. Stix showed us his Buick Invicta, which he cherished and often took for spins upstate in the country.

Marilyn showed up while we were in John's living room, mostly Kim and Maureen talking and Stix interjecting. Marilyn said little and when she did you could hardly hear her.

Then we were seated around the small, ornate dinner table, Marilyn to my left, Stix at the head flanked by Kim Stanley and Maureen, with the other actor sitting next to Kim. The space and occasion was too small for Marilyn to speak in hushed tones, but she did—leaning to the right and whispering to me. I'd nod.

With her champagne glass refilled a few times, Marilyn whispered to me at the dinner table, asking if James Dean had been "unduly lonely." I said I presumed so. She wanted to know the depth of his sadness and I said I had no way of measuring that. In a breathy, guarded voice like she'd used in *Don't Bother to Knock*, she said, "His sadness had to penetrate his soul, didn't it?" I agreed. Maureen was trying to hear what she was saying, and Marilyn spoke in an even more secretive, hushed tone. "He was sent away and had no one," she said. "He was on the same train with the coffin that contained his own mother's body..."

Ray told me Marilyn knew even then—before hitching up with "egghead" Arthur Miller that same year, that she'd never have a kid—

Catholic, Jew, or otherwise. As much as she tried, she feared it would never be a reality. She told Susan she had a dream that she'd given birth to a dead baby.

"She was practically afraid of everything," Susan said. "I don't know who she really trusted or what she trusted to any extent beyond something to do with her own best interest—that of being in front of the camera. You can't blame Marilyn. That's what we were all after...But I can't even say she trusted herself, religiously seeking advise from everyone, then only to follow her own instincts, and these were often a mess of contradictions...

"Her concept of a role was put together as a singular experience. She rarely communicated with other actors above addressing them as cue cards."

Kim Stanley said, "Marilyn related to what she understood and experienced in an instinctual way, and this she translated to her exterior presentation. She'd give her best, no matter how long it took her, and while the work we were doing at the Studio wasn't really related to what Marilyn was doing, what she did was something no one else seemed able to do. Lee (Strasberg) told us to appreciate her, to show our appreciation. He wanted her to feel that we were all cheering for her, and to let Marilyn know by our appreciation that we were her friends and we cared. He said she needed that confidence. In so many words, he said she was an important contribution to the work we doing, but frankly, I didn't see that. She seemed *extremely* sensitive and if you looked at her the wrong way she'd be crushed and depressed...

"No one had Marilyn's beauty or the childlike quality or innocence she possessed. It didn't matter that what you were asked to appreciate was an abstract, by that I mean apart from a performance we usually understood. Marilyn was on her own, and perhaps in that lies the tragic quality that emanated from her projection of innocence—a girl who had never grown up or was *allowed* to grow up. She had the beauty few of us have, and the magic we dream about, and somehow it could radiate truthfully from the rather surface approach she had to a performance. That she didn't understand it doesn't make a difference. She knew how to use what she was doing and her work was almost totally surface because she hadn't the tools to tap into herself and bring forth true emotion. Maybe she didn't want to. I personally believe it was a terrible place she dreaded entering. So she resisted any such attempt. It was only what the camera saw that mattered and that's when she came to life. Frankly, few have ever done it better."

Susan said, "Marilyn was completely unique and she was my friend. She derived nothing from someone else because her worries made her gun-shy of others. She was afraid she didn't fit in and carried this conflict throughout her life which was a history of emotional deprivation that saturated her soul..."

A Studio member, Clint Kimbrough, told me he believed few understood Marilyn because they only grabbed what they could and fawned over the fact of having made contact with Marilyn Monroe. "She was probably the most unfortunate companion you could know," Clint said, "because you were always dealing with two people. One was the movie star, and then the other one—that private self, played this game of keeping you at bay.

"I think she *wanted* someone to understand her, but I don't think she knew what she expected them to understand, like she'd place that responsibility in their hands. There could be a difficult time communicating with her and I think that is where the tragic part comes in that Kim Stanley talked about.

"Marilyn would always resist revealing what she really was, like the Studio preached endlessly—finding the real self, projecting *this* through the work, not a surface caricature. This is what you projected— what made you in*volved* in the work. She was on drugs and that's like oil and water. You walk around like James Dean said in *Rebel Without a Cause,* that you had your head in a sling. She'd never show her real self, but everyone was appreciating that she was a part of the Studio anyway. No secret she was headliner for Actors Studio.

"Downers and booze that kept her mellowed out, and then the need for more and more was the chance she took—or anyone takes. I was told she was on medication, a tranquilizer called Thorozene. I don't think anyone knew exactly how serious her drug problem was and maybe some of her best work was in covering what was happening inside herself...

"I think she was getting lost fast," Clint said. "The more successful she was becoming, the more she was losing her way. I worked with her adopted sister—I guess that's what you'd call her—Jody Lawrance, in the picture *Hot Spell* with Anthony Quinn. Shirley Booth played my mother. Jody's real name was Nona Goddard, and she'd been raised for a time with Marilyn. She told me Marilyn—who'd been called Norma Jeane back then, was taking strong pills since she was eighteen years old because of these terrible menstrual periods. Nona said Marilyn couldn't stop bleeding sometimes and she was in awful pain. So she was on pain killers and sleeping pills back then and it seems she never never got off it."

By '59, Marilyn was seriously addicted. She had stayed at a peak level of downers mixed with alcohol through the work she did, but the intake only increased. On screen, her work with other actors *appears* a blended union, but in reality it was segmented, linked only by skillful editing. So many takes, so repetitious with Marilyn's attempts to "get it right," then somehow with a coach's approval, she knew when a take was successful. It didn't matter if fellow performers or crew suffered exhaustion or frustration, fearing the worst for themselves, having found it a near-impossibility to repeat so many takes of the same simple scene and to appear their best through the exhausting process of working with Marilyn.

Her lateness created a general atmosphere of anger, and from the start she was like an anxious creature threading through a swarm of determined hornets. Full of fear and oppressed by furious directors, maligned by most crew and actors, Marilyn often fled rather than confront, cried rather than listened. She'd wrap herself inwards—numb the panic with pills and cry, "Everyone hates me!" She'd say, "I'm sorry but I can't make it better for anyone else!"

She'd crafted a shield against outside interference. Regardless of the disappointment and wounded feelings she would cause others, Marilyn would say, "This is the way I have to *do* something! Why can't anyone understand what *I* have to do?"

Ralph Roberts was always on hand to massage the tension from her shoulders, knead the pains in her neck and arms and ease the iron-like stress from between her shoulder blades. "She'll get sick before a scene," he said, "almost every scene. She knows they're calling her and everyone is mad at her, but she'll be vomiting because she is afraid to go out and go to work, and no one can do anything about it."

Ralph Roberts

I recall Roberts saying, "She almost always gets literally sick before she has to get on the set, which causes her to be late, so what she does, she takes pills to calm her and then a drink of something..."

While Marilyn's image blossomed and thrived on film, she grew more terrified of personal exposure. She said, "Everyone is looking at me and I can't look at them..." She believed they'd be seeing *inside* of her, her "personal self," yet she was confused further because she didn't know what she feared might be exposed. Each agonizing minute of performing rented into her like the beaks of a bunch of hawks. She told John Stix in New York that she once dreamed when she was making *Gentleman Prefer Blondes* that a swarm of little birds flew in her face and tried to peck out her eyes.

Looking thinner and sleepless, her glances darting, Marilyn told Rory Calhoun it was like "being called before a firing squad." Or they were going to run over her "in a big car..." Everyone would be on the sidelines viewing the accident.

The wall she erected around herself was constructed so tightly there wasn't room to accommodate another. She begged for advice and counsel, and paid plenty for it, but listened only to her "inner senses."

"Her face would be blotched red," Richard Allan said about shooting *Niagara,* "her neck and chest breaking out in nervous rashes... I'd think about Ava Gardner, having worked with her, and how smoothly she went into a scene, almost gliding into it, and then how opposite Marilyn was from this. It was very strange. She was *really* afraid, and half the time in terrible pain and unable to work. A disastrous situation when you're making a movie and every delay costs a fortune. I really didn't understand what it was. The studio said it was psychosomatic — not that some of it wasn't, but the worst of it was not a psychological reaction but a physical condition she couldn't help. She was frail and never very well."

With an elevation in pain came the escalation of drugs. Allan said, "One time she told me she'd been cursed. I found that one of the most extraordinary things she said — that she'd been *cursed*. And she was saying in her heart she could do nothing about it..."

To block the pain and *appear* to have control, the answer was always at hand. Loading up on pills spiked with alcohol, she could maneuver through a scene, a sole survivor on the desert island of a movie set. She came alive through the camera that snatched her charisma as you'd pare the juiciest morsel from the rest, and that was what moviegoers saw, and all that mattered to them.

Marilyn had hinted at a congenital condition that assured infertility, and her dream of having a family would remain nothing more than a dream. Though she'd try again and again to get pregnant, without enjoying the process (she'd told Monty Clift, "I hate sex — it makes me sick..."), Marilyn would leave miscarriages in her path.

"Being a most serious actress," she once told Susan, "is not something *God* has removed from my destiny as He chooses to destroy my chances of being a mother. It's therefore my prerogative to make the dream of creative fulfillment come true. That is what I believe God is saying to me and that must be the answer to my prayers...

"They can suspend me and try to sue me until they are blue in the face," she said, "but a person must do what they believe they are summoned by destiny to do..."

There it was, all wrapped up in pink tissue paper with ribbons around it, like Fred MacMurray says in *Double Indemnity*.

Diana Herbert and Sherman Billingsly

Spies on 58th Street

Diana Herbert, after several years of Broadway and television, married Larry Markes, a hotshot TV writer for Steve Allan and Jack Parr. They were living in the East 60s, but Diana was hanging out at Sardi's with actor and ex-boyfriend Sam Levine—or Ralph Meeker or Bob Webber. They were, she says, "wonderful, intense, romantic relationships, and then I had to set them aside because I wanted a family." She was also pregnant.

"Sam and I had done a Broadway show, fallen in love and even talked about getting married. Of course it didn't work out, but Sam and I stayed close friends. We'd talk about shows, though since I'd gotten pregnant I pretty much was side-stepping getting on stage. I remember in Sardi's talking about Marilyn and how much Fox was bringing in on *The Seven-Year Itch*, then Sam saying he understood the situation she'd had with Johnny Hyde—trading sex for a trip to the moon. 'That's not how the game goes,' I said, 'and you damn well know it, Sam.' I said you live in Hollywood half your life, you accept how the game's played. Sam was smiling and said something about a rose under any other name. We both laughed."

Sex in Hollywood is part of the game—an exchange that has never altered since old silent cameras were cranking on one-wall sets. The reality of being a name player is that relationships or marriages last about as long as a movie and end as fast. Living in the shade of the industry,

Sam Levine and Diana

many often fail to shake the acting persona in their off-camera lives. When they do, they're scrambling to hold a consistent identity. You're playing your part in the game.

"Growing up in Hollywood," said actor Bobby Blake, a friend for a number of years, "you learn life's different from your pappy's farm like in the middle of Wisconsin or Kalamazoo. People come out here to Hollywood, to whore themselves thinking they'll get in a movie. They can whore themselves the same in Wisconsin or Kentucky as the Hollywood whores, but none of them get into pictures. They just end up being whores."

Blake said the game played in Tinseltown is make-believe because so few are able

Ralph Meeker and Diana

to invest any *real* emotional substance in sustaining a relationship, whether a hit-and-run marriage or a weekend in Acapulco or Palm Springs. Every-thing is expendable except the gratification of getting yourself on the giant movie screen. "That's the heart you go straight at," says Blake, "the prize in the box of Cracker Jacks, and each relationship is a rung on a ladder to getting up there and grabbing that prize."

Elia Kazan was quick to describe Marilyn as "a simple, decent-hearted kid whom Hollywood brought down, legs parted," though he neglected to confess his part in spreading her legs. A key player in using a user, Kazan got what he was after, but Marilyn, who half-heartedly claimed to have fallen for Kazan enough to compose love poems, didn't get a movie out of one of the world's great directors. What Kazan did, inadvertently, was put her pretty toenail-painted feet a few rungs up the ladder.

Diana Markes nee Herbert says, "I was eight months pregnant as all get out when I ran into Marilyn by the subway entrance on 58th Street. I said, 'Marilyn!' and she looked around confused and nervous at my calling her out of the blue. You wouldn't have known it was her the way she had herself covered up with that scarf and sunglasses. I said, 'Scudda hoo! Scudda hay!' Then she grabbed my hand and asked me who I was. I said, 'I'm *Diana*, for God's sake,' and I sang a line from *I Never Took a Lesson in My Life*.

"She said, 'But you're pregnant! Look at you—you're so pregnant,' and I said, 'Well, I *hope* so!' She asked if I could feel the baby moving inside myself, and I said, 'well, yeah,' and she could too. I placed her hand on me and she jumped a little, saying, 'Oh! The baby kicked my hand.'

"Minutes later she led me half a block over by Carnegie to a little, tiny Greek restaurant. They had a couple tables and we sat in the corner where it was the darkest. I told her I'd changed my diet and was sticking close to food that was good for me and the baby. I guess we talked and then a tear ran down her cheek from under the sunglasses. She said she admired me so much and was so envious it was making her cry. She removed the sunglasses and wiped her eyes, then asked if she could feel the baby again.

"We had coffee and a little something, a kind of Greek cake, but she kept looking out the window at the street and I asked if she was expecting someone, which I assumed was the reason she'd hurried me to that particular restaurant. She said, 'No one I *want* to be expecting.' I didn't know what she meant, and she said, 'They're spies.' I said, 'Spies? What spies?' She got a funny look and for just an instant I thought, my God, maybe Marilyn's gone off the deep end...

"She stared at me closely and said, 'You must not say anything, but there are federal agents following me.'

"'Federal agents?' I said. Marilyn said it was the FBI, because of Arthur's past affiliations with people the agents considered to have connections to communists. 'They think he's still associated with subversives,' she said, 'and now that I am with him they suspect I'm a subversive of some sort...' I said 'If that's true, Marilyn, it's idiotic.' Then I said, 'You're not, are you?' She said of course not and agreed it was idiotic but told me she had to watch her-

The macine that makes the sound of Niagra Falls

self. Slyly, she said she'd become adept at giving them the slip. I asked, 'How long has this been going on?' *Months*, she said. I was shocked. She said a young actor told her he'd been questioned because he sympathized with liberal elements that the FBI said were associated with leftist sympathizers. 'They'd put him in a car like he was a criminal and made him show them places where he'd been and they wanted to know if Arthur had been there, and if *I* had been with him.' The actor, she said, told her they'd questioned him about Arthur and about her, and what connection she had with any associations through Arthur."

Diana said the entire thing sounded ridiculous. "Marilyn was sniffling again and kept a hankie against her nose. She said I was so blessed to be having a baby, and she'd wanted a baby more than anything. She said if she could have a baby it would change her life, and I said, 'You will, Marilyn, it'll happen. Give it time—' She said no, she didn't think she could have a baby. For a second I thought she was saying getting pregnant and having a child would interfere with her career, which it would, and I was about to tell her how I felt, but she said, 'I'll tell you something you must never ever repeat' and 'please,' and did I promise? I said of course. If I told anyone, she said, 'it would become a fucking circus...' I swore it would go no further than the coffee cup...

"She said she had a problem that caused her severe pain and

anguish—'for years,' she said, and 'there's nothing I can do about it...' It was the reason she was sick and couldn't have a family. The reason for so many problems in her life and I was so fortunate to be a 'normal' person. She said her life was not normal, and it never would be and all she could do about it was to try and stop the pain..."

Marilyn excused herself and disappeared into the little rest room. "She was gone perhaps twenty minutes to half an hour," says Diana, "and that reminded me of when she'd hid in our pool dressing room back in Bel Aire. When she came back to the table, she'd rearranged her scarf, carefully covering most of her hair."

Diana asked if Marilyn was feeling better, and the answer was a hushed but emphatic "*No!*"

"I was flabbergasted by what she'd been saying about the FBI," Diana says, "and all the personal pain she was enduring, but there was more to come. I asked if she'd seen specialists and had they told her she couldn't get pregnant? She said she'd had medical examinations 'with the kitchen sink thrown in for good measure.' She told me the problem started 'a long time ago' with her early menstrual cycles, and it was to a point where all she could think about was some way to alleviate the pain."

What *was* the problem? Diana asked, but Marilyn wouldn't say. "She seemed afraid," Diana says. "Kept looking around, and towards the street, and then she said, 'You know who is behind this, don't you?' I wasn't sure what she was saying but then she said, 'That dirty old man, *Winchell!*'

"*Walter* Winchell?" Diana asked. Of course Marilyn was saying Walter Winchell. "'Who else?' Marilyn said, 'He's the one responsible for the FBI following us!' Winchell's daughter, she said, was a 'compulsive Lesbian' and Winchell had made overtures about wanting to discuss his daughter, but then he made advances to Marilyn—even while Marilyn was sick and in pain. 'It's Winchell,' Marilyn said, 'who personally talked to J. Edgar Hoover.'"

At first, says Diana, "I was alarmed and I have to say kind of frightened how Marilyn seemed or what was eating her, and I wasn't convinced that she hadn't become a little mentally unbalanced by all the pressure she was under... I just didn't know..."

Not only was Marilyn hitting the bull's eye with her accusation about Winchell, but she had been bleeding internally as she sat admiring Diana Markes and feeling her pregnant belly.

What few knew was that Marilyn was "scared sick" that she had "some kind of cancer..." Each bowel movement caused Marilyn to lose blood. She'd told a New York internist, "Every time I sit on the toilet to do my business, I have blood coming out of me..."

She didn't have cancer, she was told. She was suffering from ulcerative colitis, no doubt brought on by emotional stress. Losing weight, her aching wrists and ankles, bleeding from the rectum, feeling weak and unbalanced, her "hemoglobin running dangerously low," were all part of the condition.

The medication made her sick. She felt oppressed by illness and told her masseur, Ralph Roberts, "I felt so heavy at times like I'm waterlogged. I can't wake up and I can't sleep. I feel like I weigh three hundred pounds and if can't get to the bathroom in time I have an awful situation..."

An ulcerated colon wasn't the only problem plaguing Marilyn. Her inability to sustain a pregnancy, her gynecologists affirmed, was the result of an endometriosis diagnosis years before. There was no apparent cure short of surgery to remove her uterus. Marilyn was adamant—a hysterectomy was out of the question. What if some hope existed that she could sustain a pregnancy? What if some discovery was made that afforded a cure?

She had been told that half the women with the same condition were infertile. She wanted to believe she was in the other half, "the positive half." She had studied medical texts and learned that for women with this problem, tissue similar to the lining of the uterus could show up elsewhere in their bodies—the pelvic cavity, the rectum, the ovaries or fallopian tubes, the bladder, intestines or appendix. It could appear inside the vagina, or even on the skin or in the lungs and spine. These growths caused severe pain and unusually heavy periods. Marilyn lived with the fear that the condition could advance to the point that her internal organs could fuse together.

One New York gynecologist had told her the pain accompanying her menstrual cycle could "without doubt" be experienced at other, unrelated times, and could prove debilitating without sufficient medication to relieve pain.

Marilyn wanted to know if there would ever be an end to it. Would it someday go away? She was told the disease could last until after menopause, with no cure short of hysterectomy. Side by side with almost every step of her success, Marilyn endured excruciating, disabling pain in her abdomen and her lower back. Sexual intercourse was painful. Going to the bathroom was painful with bleeding and intestinal symptoms similar to what she suffered from the colitis. Her illnesses brought Marilyn close to chronic fatigue. Ralph knew this as he knew her muscles and ligaments, but apart from her doctors, few others were

aware of Marilyn's physical problems. She even tended to have asthma-like attacks and suffered allergies and eczema. There was no solution except to kill the pain—pills and injections the doctors readily prescribed, the last possible resort being a hysterectomy. The thought made her puke, as did the pills and injections.

Diana says, "I had my baby, and then I had three more—a beautiful, artistic family, but I've never stopped thinking about poor Marilyn and the baby she wanted so badly... There is so much she gave us, and so little she ever had for herself."

Through Light into Dark

Between pill parties with Milton Greene, Marilyn Monroe Productions acquired film rights to William Inge's successful play, *Bus Stop*, and in February of '56 she returned to Hollywood to begin the picture. Inge would later tell Marilyn that his play *A Loss of Roses* was being written specifically with Marilyn in mind for the leading character. The playwright suggested Marilyn might consider the role on Broadway, when the time came.

However, when the time did arrive, Arthur Miller and Lee Strasberg insisted Marilyn decline the part of side-show stripper Lila Leeds on the skids. Neither Miller nor Strasberg believed Marilyn could cope with or sustain enough concentration to carry herself through a full-length play, though Marilyn told Strasberg, "Everyone says I can do it—I can be an actress in New York as easily as Hollywood!"

Strasberg said she wasn't ready "for such an undertaking. A *film* of the play, absolutely, but this particular play could prove a catastrophe at this point in your career and in your learning process here with Actors Studio."

Nor did they want her to do *Baby Doll*, Tennessee William's movie for Warner Brothers. It was talked about but Strasberg told her, "You're not ready, Marilyn. You need another year of training with us, and then you'll be ready."

"But then they'll have already made the movie!" Marilyn said.

All three of the Strasbergs—Lee, Paula and Susan—dissuaded Marilyn despite Tennessee Williams' objections.

In '59, Tennessee Williams told me, "I would've loved Marilyn in *Baby Doll*. I *wanted* her for it but the fuckers fought me and much as I wanted Marilyn, Lee (Strasberg) was keeping Marilyn under his control—or attempting to, hoarding her for themselves. Kazan pacified me but he still refused to take my desires into consideration. If Kim (Stanley) can play an ado*lescent* Marilyn in that awful *Goddess* picture, I'd certainly say Marilyn could play a nineteen year old child-woman because that's what she is—a child-woman, all wonder and thumb-sucking and I

183

adore her. I love Marilyn. Most of these assholes trying to throw their weight are nothing but a bunch of power-hungry faggots!"

Actors Studio had Marilyn selling tickets to *Baby Doll* and doing promotional work for the production. John Stix said, "I didn't think that was right. I told them why don't you have her wearing a sandwich sign and parading Times Square..."

Shelley Winters said, "There was a lot of political shit going on in New York, and even somebody blind could've seen the importance of keeping someone as important a figure as Marilyn dependent on you if you've got some agenda for using that person..."

Paula accompanied Marilyn through the making of *Bus Stop*, salaried as Marilyn's coach. Director Josh Logan said, "I had no problem with that end of it, with Paul Strasberg on the set. She was always dressed in black and the crew called her 'Black Bart.' I had few if any of the problems other directors have faced with Marilyn. We worked well together—she is a highly creative and sensitive person, and I can only suggest that her very complex personality may arouse conflicts in other directors. I had no such problem of cracking a whip on the set...Marilyn is an intuitive individual who works intuitively to the extent that she often doesn't recognize herself in relation to others. She was remarkable."

Actor Don Murray was an unknown appearing in a Broadway play when cast by Josh Logan for *Bus Stop*. Murray says, "Logan was a very patient man and I learned a great deal from him. I believe the ultimate goal for him was what we could accomplish, and in that he gave us pretty free rein. I personally found working with Marilyn difficult at times because she had trouble remembering lines and her concentration was off. We'd do as many as thirty takes when usually a film scene requires about five. The importance for the production was of course Marilyn's performance and with so many takes you can only hope for the best. I found her to be into herself and there was very little social interchange on the set. She seemed frightened and worried or she was nervous just trying to get things right. She did object to Hope Lange's blonde hair and it had to be darkened. I was going with Hope Lange at the time."

Murray says Paula Strasberg was continually with Marilyn, going over every line in the script, and Marilyn seemed to have placed herself in Paula's hands.

Billy Travilla had designed costumes on four of Marilyn's films before *Bus Stop*. "Marilyn's ideas," he said, "were simple, glamorous and straightforward. She felt things and her instincts were usually correct, though she didn't necessarily reason them out. She responded and I like to think we became quite close. I'd done costumes for Joan Crawford in *Flamingo Road*, in which Joan begins as a sideshow girlie dancer, and Marilyn told me excitedly that she wanted to talk to 'Miss Crawford' about the sort of character she portrayed. Marilyn told me during *Bus Stop* that this was the kind of character she was playing at the time and the kind she hoped to be playing in a new William Inge play in New York. I was surprised to hear that...

"She told me she'd wanted the Jean Peters part in *Pickup on South Street*, which I also did the costumes for. Richard Widmark had starred opposite Peters. I knew that Marilyn had badgered Fox about it though the director, Sam Fuller, had vetoed it. Nothing personal against Marilyn, simply that she wasn't 'dark' enough as the way Fuller had put it. It was a role I believe Marilyn could have done successfully, given the opportunity."

Sam Fuller wrote as well as directed *Pickup on South Street*. He told me, "It would have been such a case of putting the cart before the horse that we turned down the idea. Marilyn was too flashy, too attractive and this sort of appearance would have been incongruous. She thought it was same sort of role she had in *Don't Bother to Knock*, but the fact is that it was an entirely different character but Marilyn didn't understand that. She wanted to make faces and play a crackpot which was antagonistic to the story. No, it was a simple misconception on her part and frankly Fox had nixed Marilyn's inspired request before any of us reached the point of seriously considering her... She said something interesting to me after that, to the effect that an actor doesn't have the say-so of their own life, and was their destiny always to be dictated by the will of someone else? I remember looking at that gorgeous face and saying something like, 'I think that's how it is, Marilyn, and they're always gonna say it's nothing personal."

In June '56, with *Bus Stop* completed, Marilyn returned to New York. At the same time, Miller returned to New York after being granted a divorce in Reno, Nevada. In a civil ceremony on the 29th of June, Marilyn and Miller were married in New York. Two days later, a Jewish ceremony was held and Marilyn announced she was converting to Judaism.

As the news broke, Marilyn Monroe movies were immediately banned by the Egyptian government as well as in other Islamic countries where she'd previously been held in wonderment. "Marilyn Monroe is *outlawed*!" Egypt announced. "She has married a Jew and has become a Jew!"

Miller disliked Milton Greene and Greene felt usurped by Miller, while both milked the opportunities afforded by Marilyn. The next project, *The Prince and the Showgirl*, to be filmed in London with Sir Laurence Olivier, was the downhill path to collapse of Marilyn Monroe Productions.

Josh Logan said, "That project was potentially a nightmare from the inception. The clash between such a highly structured performer as Olivier and the fearful, frightened, intuitive Marilyn spelled doom from the start."

Olivier functioned by concept, and like Alfred Hitchcock he infused upon each scene what he had laboriously structured intellectually. There was no room for spontaneity and, unfortunately for such directors, Marilyn was a creature of pure spontaneity. She could not stick to any programmed plan of approach. Her best work stemmed from her innate sense of excitement and make-believe. Josh Logan said, "She was a wonder and we had a marvelous time on *Bus Stop*. She should have received an Oscar for her work, it was that brilliant."

Laurence Olivier told an associate, "I was hired to star in and direct this picture but I could just as easily have been repairing a kitchen sink. Marilyn was the most impossible human being I have ever worked with in my entire career. It occurred to me at one point in this mangle of chaos that the girl was absolutely crazy. She was continually in some sort of pain—physical or psychic, and the experience for the making of a motion picture was absolutely monstrous. The delays and lateness and no-shows should be jotted up in a record book... We fought from start to finish and she was so crocked half the time on drugs and drink that I could've been talking to a lamp post."

Billy Wilder, having directed Marilyn in *The Seven Year Itch* and then *Some Like It Hot,* later made a statement about her that is worth repeating. He said, "She was an absolute genius as a comedic actress, with an extraordinary sense for comedic dialogue. It was a God-given gift. Believe me, in the last fifteen years there were ten projects that came to me, and I'd start working on them and I'd think, 'It's not going to work, it needs Marilyn Monroe.' Nobody else is in that orbit; everyone else is earthbound by comparison."

Actor Tony Curtis, however, has a different view. "Whatever pains she might've had," he says about the making of *Some like it Hot*, "were mild compared to the aches in the ass she caused everyone else. I'm saying she hung us up for hours—days," says Curtis. "Billy [Wilder] did all he could to instill in her a sense of professional responsibility but it was to no avail. You couldn't get through to her... She was smart—*bright*, wasn't a formal education but a native intelligence, yet she couldn't fit in with the people in her surroundings. That's what gets me looking back now. It was play-acting—her brightness was twisted at the bases, and I loved her but she was a monster plain and simple. I'm not exaggerating, and God forgive me, but I can't help facing the bitter truth of it. Her attitude was inappropriate with everyone. Wouldn't come out of the dressing room. What the fuck's she *doing* in there? We're waiting—*waiting* like wooden props. Like we've got no lives, you know. Everything around her suffered because of her attitude. Making a *show* of what a monster she could be so we're all as miserable as she is. I said to her, 'If this is such a pain the ass, why don't you quit the business and go into Russian or Nazi politics?' She said back to me, 'Oh, Tony, what on earth do you *mean* by that?'"

Co-star Jack Lemmon said, "I talked to her. I tried to get her to get control of things in the hope of getting through the picture. Okay, she gave a performance that was tantamount to sheer brilliance, but we had a *trying* schedule and it was practically impossible for her to stick to it. I had a life apart from the damned picture but it became increasingly apparent to me that Marilyn didn't. See, she didn't have a life apart from being in pictures, and getting close enough to her to make a difference was an exercise in futility. I mean, what the hell, you're doing it for overall good of the project, but Marilyn simply had *no life off the set*. She made that emptiness, if that's what it was, her prison. It had to do with her life, I believe, and how she'd lived, as I kid, I mean, and it was still living in her. It wasn't her *past*, she was carrying it around because she had no other life of her own—she hadn't matured into something other than that troubled child, and it was it was like something she had no control over... In fact, I'd say it controlled her—to a wide margin."

187

Marilyn became pregnant during the filming of *The Prince and the Showgirl*, but back in New York the pregnancy was found to be entopic as a result of the endometriosis, and would have to be aborted, she was told, in order to save her life.

Jonathan Gilmore and Regina Gleason in A Loss of Roses

A subsequent pregnancy ended in a miscarriage—her disappointment so severe she shut herself away for days in the apartment she shared with Miller. The playwright by then was wading through bad waters financially, with Marilyn's earnings keeping them afloat. The failed pregnancy struck Marilyn as some "traitorous act of fate," thus setting her on a course of refusing contact with those she knew before the London fiasco with Sir Laurence. She also gave some clear indications (hinted to Billy Travilla), that she was no longer sharing a bed with her husband, who, she let slip, might not remain her husband for "very much longer."

That seemed to be the coming scenario as soon as Marilyn and Miller returned to Hollywood for her to begin filming *Let's Make Love*, which she considered "an atrocious bunch of nothing." Jerry Wald, producing for Fox, had a second movie up his sleeve. He was planning on filming the William Inge play, *A Loss of Roses*, and said to Marilyn, "Like the old saying, what goes around comes around, right?"

Marilyn and Miller were lodged into a bungalow at the Beverly Hills Hotel, as were the Montands—the French star Yves Montand, starring opposite Marilyn in *Let's Make Love*, and his wife, the brilliant actress Simone Signoret.

Curtis Harrington, Jerry Wald's associate, says, "From the start there were problems. George Cukor was directing and doing the best he could with an otherwise dreadful script. The studio had wooed Marilyn back into the folds of playing another empty-headed dumb Dora, as Zanuck enjoyed calling blondes, and despite the fact that she'd gained too much weight and was pretty spaced out a good part of the time, she delivered a wonderful performance and her songs and dance numbers were remarkable...

"Yves Montand barely spoke English and had to learn his lines phonetically, proof of the total miscasting mentality involved in this picture, but its title accurately describes the off-set behavior of Marilyn and Montand. They began an affair immediately and there were all these sparks and rumors and innuendos going on during the picture."

Several years later, during the filming of *Games* for Universal starring Simone Signoret and directed by Curtis Harrington, the French actress spoke candidly about Montand's relationship with Marilyn. "It was predictable from the start," she said. "Yves and myself have had affairs but we have loved one another and are committed to this love. This is something Marilyn could not understand. I felt for her in my heart. She was a tragic girl on a slide and was going down, and she could not stop. Her attempts to stop herself, such as the so-called romance she undertook with Yves, was a pitiful attempt to take hold of some thing of permanence in her life. Everything was getting away from her. She could hold nothing. My heart is sick for her, but she did these things to herself. To leave my husband for such an indiscretion is for me unthinkable..."

Marilyn did not believe she was sliding downhill as quickly as Simone would suggest. She believed she had some control which she was exercising. She had Jerry Wald behind her, but it was merely a flexing—a posture. No one was paying attention to how her life was being governed except Paula Strasberg and Miller, both enjoying the fruits of Marilyn's efforts.

"Someone had to be there constantly to reassure her," Harrington says. "I'd be sitting in the screening room with Jerry (Wald) and Marilyn would be down front with Paula Strasberg and throughout the screening Paula would be stroking Marilyn and telling her how beautiful she was, how talented and wonderful she'd done a scene or a line, telling her these things again and again like a broken record. She would tell her some take would be fantastic when it obviously wasn't. It was almost embarrassing in its intimacy of seeing into Marilyn's failure at coming to terms with her life and her work, and of course one doesn't see all that on the screen. You see Marilyn as exciting and glamorous, wonderfully amusing and absolutely the perfection of beauty.

"But it was a mask—a disguise, and she was becoming as insecure as the flame of a candle in a windstorm..."

Dreams

"In so many ways," said one Fox producer, "we give a loaded gun to a child, as we took a mad person and made them a movie star."

New York writer Meade Roberts was developing a script from the Inge play, *A Loss of Roses,* for Jerry Wald, tentatively titled *A Woman of Summer*. Marilyn's interest was piqued. She'd let Wald know how "displeased" she'd been that she hadn't considered doing the play which had folded after only twenty-five performances, but felt that the film would elevate her again toward another "serious" dramatic role like the one she'd performed in *The Misfits*, following the "silly" movie with Yves Montand.

Her one-sided romance with the French actor had driven a wedge between her and Miller, who had written *The Misfits* script with John Huston directing. Marilyn and Miller struggled through the making of the picture, torn apart and barely speaking. Ralph Roberts, assisting Marilyn on the set in Reno as well as playing a small part in the picture, said, "I was so concerned about her because she'd gone off the deep end with the pills and the booze. They were drinking all the time and it was impossible to coordinate anything with Marilyn. She was half conscious most of the time. We had to literally prop her up for makeup. She couldn't sleep and when she did she couldn't wake. That had become a dangerous pattern, and the wrangling with Miller, even if it wasn't a shouting match, kept her trying to numb the pains she had..."

Marilyn was drinking champagne throughout the day and lacing it heavily with vodka. "She was sick practically the entire time," Roberts said, "but no matter how hard it was to accomplish, she is totally, absolutely brilliant on film, as is everyone in the cast."

John Huston wanted to get Marilyn off the drugs. It was Miller's responsibility, Huston said, or "the girl will be pretty soon dead."

Miller said he couldn't do it. Marilyn wouldn't listen to him. He said he'd tried a hundred times to get her off the drugs and booze but it was impossible—he said she was deaf to him. "These are her demons," he said. "I don't understand her. We have really nothing in common."

Huston said later, "I couldn't help it but I said to Arthur, 'Except her money. You've got that in common.' It was a rotten thing to say to the fellow, but it was that or walloping him one. You're in the middle of the damned picture and the star—his *wife*—is half-conscious or *un*con-scious, so wasted on dope she looked like she'd croak on us, so I said we'll get her to the hospital and have her pumped out."

The company informed the press that Marilyn had suffered a "col-lapse from exhaustion," and it was Huston's hope that after they'd had her "pumped out" she'd stay off the pills and fight the booze. She didn't.

Marilyn has a scene in the film where she runs into the wasteland and turns screaming at the men. She is alone in the long shot, shrieking in the desolate emptiness of the desert. Marilyn blamed Miller for writ-ing the scene. She said, "I could've told them how I felt, I didn't have to go berserk and scream my head off." She felt she had given a "terri-ble performance" in that scene, her rage intended to save the lives of several horses. She said, "Arthur planned it and it is clearly traitorous," when in fact it is one of the truly great, powerful cinematic moments.

Traitorous! She didn't want to open that far, to show so much. She'd lived a life of hiding, burying her fury that shrieked out on that flat plain—crying out against the traitors.

After being pumped out in the hospital, Marilyn said, "I was scared. They said I could've died in the middle of the picture. How awful that would've been for everyone…"

Arthur Kennard, an agent with Lester Salkow, advised me that Jerry Wald had penciled my name for a role in *A Woman of Summer*. I'd been recommended by Marlon Brando, Raymond Burr, and Hunt Stromberg, Jr, who was determined to star me in a television series.

Brando's close friend and associate, Sam Gilman, directed the Los Angeles production of *A Loss of Roses*, in which I'd played the boy who falls for the down-on-her-luck blonde, nine or so years older than the boy, and who attempts suicide with broken glass.

I saw Marilyn at Fox and she said she loved the story but didn't care for the script being developed by Meade Roberts. She said, "Even if Meade is supposed to be so close to Tennessee (Williams), I don't think he understands Mr. Inge's concept of this woman who is faced with an incredibly sad future. She has dreams—she only has dreams, and is liv-ing by her dreams, don't you think so?" She had started *Something's*

Got to Give, a comedy remake with Dean Martin and Wally Cox, who I knew through Sam Gilman and Brando. George Cukor was directing.

I met with Jerry Wald twice, and Curtis Harrington several times, then finally got a draft of the script. Lester Salkow was keeping channels open, and I told Arthur Kennard and Lester that I wanted to get close to Marilyn; I felt it would be an important plus for the movie if all went well. Hunt Stromberg, Jr., talked to Wald again and said I'd be the next up and coming star. He said, "I told Wald you're James Dean and Montgomery Clift rolled into one."

I saw Marilyn again on the Fox lot and she seemed confused, panicky, and unhappy. She said, "My fingernails are broken, do you see that?"

She was seeing a psychiatrist. Dr. Ralph Greenson, counselor to Beverly Hills matrons and a handful of movie personalities. Marilyn Monroe became the patient of his dreams. In a short time, Marilyn confided that since she'd been spending so much of her time with Greenson, for the first time in her life, so she said, she was able to have a sexual orgasm.

For Marilyn, the past few years of marriage to Miller had been shrouded with misery, pain, and suspicion. One source on the *inside* confirmed the FBI's tracking of Arthur Miller and Marilyn that year in New York. "Miller defied the feds. Half the time he didn't know he was being followed due to some obvious shadowing which was a blind for the inside agent who Miller knew but hadn't an inkling they were working for the other side.

"Monroe was more cagey because she was afraid of the agents and had a built-in radar and kept up a little game of hide and seek and cat and mouse until I think she lost interest or actually thought they'd let up. Of course they hadn't and the investigation accelerated when the secret service started having a lot of questions about the President crossing paths with Monroe, married to a self-stated ex-fellow traveler, if you want to call Miller that, coupled with the extremely tense and volatile world and political situation with the Russians.

"The feds knew all about the loose zipper on Kennedy's trousers and they were keeping a scorecard with the blondes on the coast and the blondes in New York. He had secret service agents running after him cleaning up the messes. Because he was a nice enough guy, to some degree, the messes with these broads never got too out of hand.

But with Monroe "it was a dalliance, and by that I don't mean any romantic relationship developing. The problem was you had the President intersecting with an ex-commie's wife, herself an avowed leftist, and then the pot of fish started stinking when Monroe flies to Mexico and gets hooked up with Fred Field, a big shot of the American Communist Party in Mexico.

"Yes, there was an agent on the plane and two more at the Mexican airport. Another pair tracked Monroe's comings and goings with Fred Field, taking down license plates and names, and lo and behold you find she'd sitting in the middle of a nest of communists. The lady who's assisted the President with his zipper on at least one occasion in Palm Springs, unless they spent the night playing mumbley-peg.

"Next, and it's pretty obvious, she's rubbing noses with a major communist in Mexico. This guy, Fred Field, was married and the three of them were all close but then when the wife wasn't around and Field was transporting Monroe, it appeared to the agents that the closeness was more than rubbing noses. This Field—a Vanderbilt, was tall and thin and looked a little like Miller, so it was speculated that she'd dumped Miller and grabbed a bigger fish—Field. The only question Hoover had, as well as the secret service, was just what was going on with Monroe's fellow traveler friends and the fact of Kennedy's loose zipper.

"But further, and most important, Hoover wanted to throw a log jamb to further political aspirations of John F. Hoover had actually said, 'I want that son of a bitch tarred and feathered.'"

Fred Field fell for Marilyn, and under the guise of decorating her first and only house in a Mexican motif, she was being escorted through a fertile "minefield of subversives," according to Hoover.

Field knew the shadow of the FBI had dimmed his relationship with Marilyn, and to protect her he arranged for a young, handsome Mexican screenwriter, Jose Bolanas, to accompany Marilyn back to the states and to make a show of affection for the American press. She told Fred, "I'll be back at Christmas, and that's a promise."

"Marilyn's drug addiction by this time," says Sam Gilman, "was way out of control and her drinking, a lethal combination with the drugs, had her practically lost to her surroundings. I mean, at this point she would look at you and not even know who you were. Marlon, who was one of the people she'd contact out of the blue—and he never had an affair with her as the press tries to postulate—said he was very upset by what Marilyn was doing to herself but nobody could help her because everyone was hauling off their chunk of her, and Marlon said there wasn't one person she could turn to—including himself."

Marilyn didn't care whether Jose Bolanas was Bolanas or a baboon in a black suit. He fawned over her, hung over her, wanted far more than Marilyn was even capable of giving. His overnight love unrequited, Bolanas found himself stranded by Marilyn and with a one-way ticket back to Mexico.

Much of Marilyn's time was spent in long sessions with Greenson. He kept writing prescriptions. She was getting injections as well as loading on Nembutal orally, first puncturing the capsules with a safety pin to accelerate the effect. She was taking chloral hydrate. Few people were seeing her. Greenson was recommending she begin to "reappraise" those on the "fringes of her life... Weed them out," he'd advised.

Jody Lawrance, Marilyn's foster-sister, whose real name was Josephine or Nona Goddard, had tried to contact Marilyn, who did not respond. She'd tried a few years before when she'd worked in *Hot Spell* with Clint Kimbrough from Actors Studio.

Rand Brooks, Marilyn's "on-screen heart throb" from *Ladies of the Chorus*, had tried to reach Marilyn, without success.

Jody had been acting for several years, was seeing about a picture at Universal, a "bit part," she'd told Clint, but work was work. She said she wanted to tell Marilyn she still thought of her as a big sister.

Marilyn didn't want to look over her shoulder. Perhaps, at this point in her life, looking back was not possible. Ten years earlier *Niagara* had opened and she'd received the Redbook Award as Best Young Box Office Personality. This was followed by the Photoplay Award as

Fastest Rising Star of 1952.

In May '52 she'd hit the ceiling of her Fox contract and was making only $1,500 per week. *Gentleman Prefer Blondes* opened in New York and premiered at Grauman's Chinese. Marilyn was at the pinnacle of what she'd dreamed of when she paraded on Saturdays and Sundays over the concrete spread of hand and footprints with Grace or sometimes Gladys at her back. Grace had stood beside her over Norma Tallmadge's footprints and said to Marilyn, "You were named after her, Norma Jeane."

Grace McKee also lost touch with Marilyn. Grace had turned fifty-five on New Year's Day '53. Time had crawled since she'd left West Virginia to return to the small house on Odessa in Van Nuys, where she'd drummed up the idea of saving Norma Jeane from two more years in an orphanage, by getting married to Jim Dougherty.

She followed Norma Jeane's unfolding fame. She saw how Marilyn Monroe was opening to success like the wings of a beautiful butterfly — she indeed had replaced Jean Harlow. Grace McKee sat slumped before a television set and drank every day. There was no other solace for her. She took barbiturates. She never saw Norma Jeane again. The movie star she looked at in magazines was someone else. Grace had told her step-daughter Nona—Jody Lawrance—that she had once sent Norma Jeane away and she could see the girl's face "as plain as day," and the look in the girl's eyes as though Grace had turned into Judas.

Still married to Ervin Goddard, she never spoke of Norma Jeane. If the subject came close, Goddard would leave the room. He drank and stayed out at nights. Around three in the morning on September 28, he returned to the house and walked into the bedroom. Around eight that evening Grace had said she was tired and hitting the sack.

Goddard found her dead. He saw the empty bottle of barbiturates with which she had taken her life.

Years later, a failed actress, Nona would take her own life.

Memories for Marilyn became dreams which she would quickly forget. What small portion of control she'd grappled to hold over her life had been surrendered to Greenson, who wrote more prescriptions. The doctor was consulted when Marilyn's behavior and actions seemed out of control to the studio on the picture with Dean Martin.

Wally Cox, as a shoe salesman in *Something's Got to Give*, said, "I loved Marilyn and I didn't side with the big chiefs but I thought they should've scrapped the picture right away when it started falling to pieces... It was kind of crazy what was going on..."

She had two pictures to do: when she finished *Something's Got to Give*, she would consider Jerry Wald's *A Woman of Summer*, with its title changing to *The Stripper*. I was personally holding to the dream that she'd do it—that she'd come through the haze she was in and make Wald's movie. But things were rolling in a different direction.

Lee Wallace says, "I couldn't understand why she didn't ask for the moon which they would've given her for *Something's Got to Give*. She'd never been nuts about doing the picture but took it on like she had nowhere else to go. It was a disaster... "

Marilyn remarked to Ralph Roberts—who was being shut out of her life at the orders of Greenson—that she was not happy. She was in a state of complete misery. She said she saw herself falling and there was nothing to stop her, as if she was clutching weeds on the side of a bluff as she slid to its bottom. She was falling alone.

The key game-player in Fox's mishaps was Elizabeth Taylor, bankrupting the studio with costs so far exceeding the budget on *Cleopatra* that the studio was sinking. An executive says, "We thought Marilyn's movie would pull in substantial returns to offset the financial disaster *Cleopatra* was causing. But you had Marilyn and you had Dean Martin—a remake soapbox picture which should've been a breeze, but because of Marilyn was quickly bringing the studio to further losses."

She was causing so much trouble with absences and delays and just refusing to cooperate that the shooting schedule had gone nuts. The brass met and it was determined that Marilyn had gone crazy. "Her mother was crazy—she's in a nut house. Marilyn's on pills and liquor and it's a losing battle. We're getting fucked from both ends."

Though it had been planned well in advance, Marilyn's trip to New York to sing "Happy Birthday" for President Kennedy in Madison Square Garden was the last straw. Due to the exorbitant delays and losses, Fox

197

forbid her to go to New York. She defied them and appeared in one of her finest moments singing to the President. It was another ride on a big pink elephant.

To cut further losses, Zanuck said, "Kill the picture now. Everyone's laid off and Marilyn is fired. She'll never work in Hollywood again!" Tell her she's dead, they said, and go get buried.

Scrambling in a frenzy of damage control, Marilyn binged on a self-promotional campaign that had brand new photographs published world-wide and extensive interviews in leading magazines. She was the biggest star in Hollywood, and the world sympathized heartedly with Marilyn. The world had not been on the movie set.

Fox reconsidered their rashness while Marilyn pranced before the cameras for magazines. Within days, a "new deal" between Marilyn and Fox was announced, and all heads came together to reach an understanding equitable to all.

For the first time in her life, Marilyn would be paid a reasonable sum under the new contract that allowed the creative freedom she so earnestly sought, while at the same time honoring new terms to make pictures she would approve of. First was the completion of *Something's Got to Give*; then two more pictures.

But the dark, like a damp fog, had settled in. Marilyn had spent months with Greenson who had now lost his attachment to her. Like a jealous lover, Greenson manipulated Marilyn's thinking and her choices. He advised the firing of her associates, cutting off the few closest to Marilyn—her "team." Ralph said, "He was having her get rid of the people who loved her and were devoted to her. No one sees a psychiatrist for hours and hours at a time and practically lives in the psychiatrist's *home*. It's sick and abnormal. He's a Svengali who's taking Marilyn away from everything so that he'll have her exclusively for himself in a bizarre mental association. It is as if he's getting into her head completely and replacing her will with his own..."

George Barris, who had been a dutiful friend to Marilyn and the last professional photographer to take pictures of her, says, "She was just out of it. She responded to questions automatically and without energy, as if reciting a newspaper article. She was drinking heavily and was obviously medicated beyond making much sense..."

Greenson was demonstrating power by giving and taking. He would lavish "psychological" attention, then withhold it. He would fawn over her, then desert her. He was testing her dependence to see how far she would reach for his reassurance. Greenson was deserting his own family as had Johnny Hyde. He had fallen into the role of DiMaggio and Miller and Fred Fields in Mexico. But even as the Svengali who had wanted to own Marilyn, to make her a puppet in his skillful hand, Greenson had failed to reach the depths of Marilyn's anguish.

It was apparent in the new deal with Fox that Marilyn's creative dream was coming true, but she could not accept the truth because she never outgrew the unworthy, neglected child who suffered an endless emptying of all that could be bestowed upon her. It was all play-acting on the surface. She believed she would be abandoned. It was an endless cycle, the same game as was being played upon her by Greenson and the others. Whoever she would place her trust in would always betray her.

She couldn't get out of bed on the morning of August 4. She had to take something to counter the leaden grip of the daily dose of the day before. She couldn't keep her eyes open yet she wasn't sleepy. It was like she was made of wood and couldn't move her legs or her arms.

She couldn't eat. She'd try to sleep more. The rest of the day she took Nembutals and spent several hours with Greenson. She was getting glimpses of the game he was playing and she said she would soon end the sessions. She took several more Nembutals. By two o'clock she could barely speak. Her mouth wouldn't move. She drank several cups of coffee but countered the caffeine with champagne. She could hardly speak over the phone. She couldn't grab the words she wanted to say. Sick of trying, she hung up the phone. It rang and she answered but the words were still out of reach.

They would become more and more out of reach as the hours passed. More than once she had to lie down. She couldn't move. When she spoke, she only mumbled. She wondered if she was dying. If she was dying, it would be like sleeping except her heart would stop beating. She knew there was a kind of electrical impulse to do with the heart that was governed by nature. It could cease like a light when the cord was pulled.

More phone calls, but she could not understand what was being said to her. Nobody could help her.

Marilyn was alone and remained alone. Sometime between midnight and four in the morning, her heart stopped beating.

Described by the *Sydney Morning Herald* as the "quintessential L.A. noir writer," John Gilmore has been acclaimed internationally for his hard-boiled true crime books, his literary fiction and Hollywood memoirs. As one of today's most controversial American writers, Gilmore's following spans the globe from Hong Kong to his native Hollywood. He has traveled the road to fame in many guises: kid actor, stage and motion picture player, painter, poet, screenwriter, low-budget director and novelist. After heading the writing program at Antioch University, Gilmore taught, traveled, and lectured extensively while producing an indelible mark in crime literature with *Severed: the True Story of the Black Dahlia*, and *L.A. Despair: A Landscape of Crimes & Bad Times*. Gilmore now lives in the Hollywood hills where he is at work on a novel and another exploration into true crime.

Send in the Clowns

In 1956, Confidential magazine published a cover story by "Bob" Slatzer, showing the snapshot he'd had taken of himself posing with Marilyn, the article entitled, *The Ordinary Joe Sure Made Time On that Couch with Marilyn Monroe!*

Slatzer not only describes sexual relations with Marilyn while she is on the phone with Joe DiMaggio, but claims his "conquests" occurred earlier, in '52 at the General Brock Hotel in Niagara Falls, Ontario.

When aware of the article, Marilyn was mortified. She couldn't understand why someone she never knew was saying such things about her. She was advised to ignore such "trash" and it would go away. "Marilyn," she was told, "For*get* it! Let the studio handle it." No one handled it.

Writer Norman Mailer wasn't going to forget it. He waited until Marilyn was dead before launching his masturbatory chest-beating scenario of Monroe's legend, his fantasy based upon a previous crackpot's short publication two years after Marilyn's death. The crackpot was Frank Capell, a rabid anti-communist friend of Walter Winchell who underwrote whatever barb against the Kennedys could be dug up or *made* up. Capell's tale ushered in the notion that Robert Kennedy and his "Gestapo team" deliberately caused the death of Marilyn. The details of Capell's "distorted, fanatic point of view" is outlined in Donald Spoto's excellent biography on Marilyn.

"Capell told me his theory," said the chairman of the Hollywood chapter of the John Birch Society, "but he lacked any concrete proof. He said Marilyn was indeed a Communist sympathizer under constant surveillance by the FBI, and he said Arthur Miller had been shadowed by the FBI, at Director Hoover's orders. Miller and

Monroe attended suspicious meetings. Capell also said he'd told his speculations personally to Walter Winchell. It seemed to me he was seeking support from any patriotic group that would appreciate his observations."

Mailer snatched Capell's scenario and deliberately pressed the tale to stir a controversy: that Marilyn was murdered by FBI and CIA agents who resented her supposed affair with Robert Kennedy. Mailer's publishers, Grossett & Dunlap, fired the volley of fake facts to the public and promoted the book to best seller status.

Then, hot on the trail of Mailer's publicity, came Robert Slatzer, an ear tuned to Mailer's jingling pockets. Despite that later, a regretful but unconvincingly sorrowful Mailer admitted he avoided researching Monroe's death because he wanted to create the "controversy" in order to sell books—he needed the money, Slatzer, undaunted, pressed forward, elaborating on Mailer's fabrication as well the concocted tale of right-wing Capell's whose ruminations were the first to dump on the Kennedys.

Slatzer never knew Marilyn before or after arranging to have his picture taken with her. No other connection or crossing of paths occurred between Marilyn and Slatzer. His bold-faced lies about someone he never knew took a serious turn when he decided to capitalize on Mailer's success.

Those journalists, biographers, and pop culture writers who have interviewed and quoted Slatzer are as guilty at propagating the fantasies as Slatzer and Mailer, and simply add fuel to the fakery.

As an author in the early 1970s, I was represented for a time by the Shepherd Literary Agency, located in the Taft Building at Hollywood and Vine. Robert Slatzer was also a client of the Shepherd Agency, and occupied a broom-closet office in the same building.

Shepherd had been selling action paperbacks by another writer, published successfully by Pinnacle Books. The publisher at Pinnacle, Dave Zintner, and his senior editor, Andrew Ettinger, were negotiating with Shepherd for a book by me as well. Shepherd was also handling negotiations on a movie script I had been hired to write, plus a deal with Pyramid Books for a memoir by me on James Dean.

Planning to cash in with his own take on Marilyn—continuing the murder conspiracy theory the public was buying as proposed by Mailer, Slatzer brandished the Niagara snapshot as "proof" of his "sex life with Marilyn," and his "first-hand authority of telling the story from the horse's mouth," meaning Marilyn's mouth.

The agent was well aware of my past acquaintance with Marilyn and my reluctance to address the subject. I was not partial to writing about her—a subject I wondered if I would ever bring out of myself.

Meanwhile, Slatzer was sketching his make-believe relationship with Marilyn which he claimed had "gone on for years, even before she started making movies." I found it absurd, and declined to share information with Slatzer.

Since he was far from an accomplished writer, another Shepherd client, ex-newspaper reporter Will Fowler, was engaged to ghost Slatzer's story and take home a percentage of the profits. The agency was handing the estate of Fowler's father, Gene Fowler, author of *Goodnight, Sweet Prince.*

Newsman that he was, Will Fowler quickly scanned the pile of assorted clippings and press Slatzer had cut and pasted into a bulky wad of "yesterday's news," and said, "This you wrap fish in. You've got nothing but clippings that everyone has and no proof at all that you knew Monroe or that she ever told *you any*thing about herself." With a laugh, Fowler walked out, tossing back, "Too bad you hadn't married the broad—we'd have a story to write."

Almost overnight, Slatzer claimed to recall that "in fact" he had been married to Marilyn, but it had "slipped" his mind. He told the agency, "Me and Marilyn took a drive to San Diego, see, and spent a night in a hotel and then we got married..."

Always a glib, alcoholic, spur of the moment name-dropper and tall-tale-teller, Slatzer began drumming up his hot-air ruminations of a past with Marilyn, lumping together the invented details of an alleged marriage and "romance" before and after the "wedding in San Diego..." an incident the entire Hollywood community was totally ignorant of. Slatzer hired a Hungarian wannabe actress to "research" the incident which Fowler would later say was, "to find some hard-to-prove-or-disprove setting for this burlesque he was putting together."

Then Slatzer announced, "It wasn't San Diego where we got married. It was in Mexico because I remember we drove across the border that weekend..." He claimed he had no memory of the exact date or location, but that it was, "Sometime in the early fifties."

"You have to be specific," he was told. "You can't say you married someone but can't remember when it was or where it took place." He said he would try to remember. A deal was on the table with Pinnacle for a "hot story on Monroe like Norman Mailer's, and the all the mysterious circumstances of her *murder*."

After some quick checking, Slatzer claimed to recall the marriage taking place "the first week in October of nineteen-fifty-two." He said it was the first weekend in October. But no, Slatzer didn't have a copy of a marriage license. He said that was lost years ago. "After all," he said, "the marriage only lasted a few days because the story would've hit and nobody wanted to see that, so it got annulled." He said he "had to" drive back to Mexico and "pay off the Mexicans to keep it quiet." Did he have any names? The attorney? Anyone? No. He didn't. What about a witness to the marriage?

He thought it over and later Slatzer produced a punch-drunk ex-boxer he knew from some stunt work in a B-movie. The vague fighter was ready to swear to being a witness to the wedding—as long as he got paid for his services. In truth he had trouble recalling where he'd been the last twenty years of his life.

Fowler said, "I could smell this foul deal a mile off and I backed out. I said, 'But you guys can use some back up in case the shit hits the fan.'"

The book was drummed together and sold to Pinnacle. The work went night and day with Slatzer whipping together the kind of tale the publisher was eager to get into circulation on the tail of Mailer's publicity.

Shit never hit the fan because the public swallowed the tale like yesterday's chicken, and while blowing his Monroe publicity even bigger, padding his already imaginary life with Marilyn, Slatzer participated in another book with Shepherd, this time trashing Bing Crosby who Slatzer claimed to have known because he had a picture taken on a golf course with Crosby. Slatzer had a number of photos of celebrities he claimed to know intimately, yet none of them knew Slatzer. The sad truth about Slatzer, who is so often quoted by so-called Marilyn historians, was that he was an alcoholic, compulsive, pathological liar who had turned his sickness to profit.

The Hollow Man, the Crosby book, was also published by Pinnacle which was eager for more. Another "good friend" of Slatzer's stepped up onto the target line—this time John Wayne. During the whipping together of this book, *Duke,* supposedly an "inside" look at Wayne, it became painfully obvious to Shepherd, the agent, and hard-writing pack-mule of the duo, that Slatzer had no more "in" to Wayne than he'd had to Crosby or Marilyn Monroe.

In time, their search for primary research turned up Wayne's remarkable makeup man, Dave Grayson. The artist was pumped for so many details, he soon got wise to the game. Grayson told Slatzer, "You guys have got nothing except me, and if you want my story you'll have to make me a co-author on the book and split the money." Otherwise, Grayson said, he'd have to go to Wayne with the truth. Shepherd, not only the guts of the duo but the brains as well, agreed with Grayson who quickly became a co-author on *Duke.*

Slatzer's tale of life with Marilyn was published and in time he sold the film rights for a TV movie produced under the title, *Marilyn and Me*. He boasted to me of "raking in fifty grand" for the movie that even portrayed Marilyn and Slatzer in Zanuck's office, the mogul sympathetic to their "romantic involvement," but insisting for the sake of Marilyn's career that the marriage be annulled.

At the time the made-for-TV movie was viewed, conspiracies were emerging in legions, including one from a would-be actress, also quoted by the so-called historians, claiming a long-spanning friendship with Marilyn. As with Slatzer, not a single shred of concrete connection could ever be substantiated.

Yet Slatzer stayed busy, thrusting himself into the limelight like a sweaty wrestler struggling between the ropes, enlisting any support for his continued "investigation into the mysterious murder death of Marilyn..." Any media source showing curiosity in Slatzer's theories and proclamations became fodder for the "cause"— demanding a new investigation into the "mystery" death.

Again, fortunately for the memory of Marilyn, all such investigative plans have collapsed under insufficient legal momentum.

However, an undaunted Slatzer continued to grapple the ropes of reason while the historians, reporters and biographers shoved every conceivable conspiracy theory into the media like Japanese cops packing a crowded subway.

Each year the tales arrive, crackpot, culture fanatic, sociologist, armchair psychologist, all stirring the stew of fantasies into a gray glue that has almost totally obscured the actual person who was Marilyn—transmogrified into a Saint Marilyn, whore goddess of the quick-buck journalists. The respected ones have limped the lying Slatzer and other fabulists beneath their arms as totems of truth, selling their fictions and exaggerations, their conspiracy theories or spinning innuendos for a gullible, scandal-hungry public—including "UFOs and Marilyn" which has wormed into the melee. The flames stay fanned by checkbook biographers like Donald Wolfe who described himself to me as "a nutcase," and who in his fabrications appears to thrive on crucifying-in-death such legendary women like the tragic Hollywood murder victim, Elizabeth Short, known as the Black Dahlia—who, like Marilyn, remains an iridescent source of brightness in the dark of a time long gone.